SCIENCE FAIRS AND PROJECTS K-8

A Collection of Articles Reprinted From

Science and Children
Science Scope
The Science Teacher

NATIONAL SCIENCE TEACHERS ASSOCIATION

First Edition—1984
Second Edition—1985

ISBN 0-87355-071-4

Introduction

Science fairs have become somewhat of an American tradition. For a brief time each year those familiar poster displays appear in classrooms and school gymnasiums across the nation, affording young scientists the opportunity to share their interests with parents, relatives, and neighbors. Erupting volcanoes, styrofoam planets, seashell collections, stop smoking posters, and gerbils in mazes stand next to experiments with plants and solar energy. They have become part of the tradition. For many students the science fair will be the culmination of hard work and persistent investigation; it may mean the beginning of a life-long fascination with science.

For me the fascination has continued. My student science project helped me to understand scientific methods and the joy one feels at the moment of discovery. As a teacher, I learned right along with my students in discovery after discovery. The rewards have always been there, and science projects became integral to my teaching of critical thinking and process skills.

Yet science projects and science fairs are not popular with everyone and with good reason. The science fair tradition includes unfair judging procedures, forced participation, and overzealous parental involvement. Poorly planned science fair activities have detracted from the science curriculum. Worst of all, some students have been discouraged by participating in science fairs.

So, what are the solutions? How can a teacher ensure a successful and rewarding science fair? Planning, of course, is essential. NSTA has assembled this collection of reprints from *Science and Children* and *The Science Teacher* to assist teachers in organizing a science fair, working with students, and establishing equitable judging procedures. Suggestions are offered for involving young children as well as high school students in projects appropriate to each. An open letter helps parents guide their children in selecting and carrying out investigations.

Keep in mind as you read through these articles that not all authors agree on the methods for organizing a science fair. Ultimately, you will have to decide what you hope to achieve, who will participate, how the fair will be organized, and how projects should be judged (if at all). Be assured that a successful fair requires much effort, but the rewards are everlasting. Wouldn't it be great to discover that one project this year has sparked a student's life-long fascination with science?

Barry A. VanDeman
Educational Services
   Coordinator
Chicago Museum of Science
   and Industry

NSTA Position Statement on Science Fairs

The National Science Teachers Association recognizes that many kinds of learning experiences, both in and beyond the classroom and laboratory, can contribute significantly to the education of students of science.

With respect to science fair activities, the Association takes the position that participation should be guided by the following principles: (1) student participation in science fairs should be voluntary; (2) emphasis should be placed on the learning experience rather than on competition; (3) participation in science fairs should not be made the basis for a course grade; (4) science fair activities should supplement other educational experiences and not jeopardize them; (5) the emphasis should be on scientific content and method; (6) the scientific part of the project must be the work of the student; (7) teacher involvement in science fairs should be based upon teacher interest rather than on external pressures or administrative directives; and (8) if a science fair is to be undertaken, such an assignment should be a replacement for one of the teacher's current responsibilities, and not an additional duty.

The National Science Teachers Association's Position Statement on Science Fairs was approved by the NSTA Board of Directors in 1968. This position statement is intended as a guide, and does not reflect the whole range of interest of our members.

Table of Contents

A FAIR EVALUATION

THE PARENTS' ROLE

BEYOND THE SCIENCE FAIR

The Nuts and Bolts of Science Fairs

Barry A. VanDeman
Philip C. Parfitt

The date for the science fair has been set. The auditorium has been booked. And you are the head of this project. Now what happens? Momentary panic, for one thing, but, when you recover from that, the questions take over. Who's going to answer them?

In fact, there are many sources of help, and the articles collected in this volume will point you toward some of them.

1. Is there more than one kind of science fair project?

Almost any science topic can be the basis for a science fair project. And the possible approaches are also numerous:

models, collections, demonstrations, hobbies, and experiments are displayed each year at science fairs across the nation. Any of these approaches can help a child learn certain science content and science skills. What type or types you encourage (or allow) at your fair will depend on your science goals. Norman F. Smith (page 42) suggests five categories of projects and recommends one category, investigative projects, to teach critical thinking and problem solving skills. On the other hand, Margaret McNay (page 30) argues in favor of projects allowing children to explore topics that sincerely interest them even if these topics do not lend themselves to an investigative approach.

2. How can I help my students select science fair topics?

Perhaps the most difficult part of doing a science project is selecting a topic and,

if necessary, formulating the question to be answered. Take some time to work with students early in the year. Introduce them to possible topics—and give them practice in asking useful questions. Stephen C. Blume (page 29) and Gail Foster (page 26) share thoughtful approaches to helping children select topics for investigation. And Bob Burtch (page 24) offers a list of possible topics.

3. By what criteria should projects be judged?

That depends on the nature of the project. Each project should be judged by criteria specific to itself. Models, for instance, should not be judged by the criteria used to judge experiments. Several articles offer sound advice. See Lawrence J. Bellipanni, et al (page 36); Harvey Goodman (page 41); Margaret McNay (page 30); Norman F. Smith (page 42).

4. Should students be required to do science projects?

In general, students should not be required to do projects if competition and awards are part of the fair. Science projects should encourage students to explore areas of science they are interested in. Forcing them, at the same time, to compete with classmates can turn off the very interest in science that the fair is designed to encourage. When the fair is not competitive, projects might be a regular class assignment, used to teach science skills while allowing for student preferences. See Evelyn Streng (page 22).

5. Should students receive awards for projects?

This is up to you. Some teachers offer certificates of participation to all student exhibitors. Others give first, second, and third place ribbons or certificates. Still others award trophies to outstanding projects. We recommend that every student receive an award or acknowledgement of participation. See Bob Burtch (page 23), Deborah C. Fort (page 10), and Evelyn Streng (page 22).

6. In what ways can the librarian help my students?

Librarians can offer lots of help if they are familiar with your standards for researching projects and writing reports. Several months before you send students out to do research, talk with the school librarian and the public librarian. Explain your science fair goals and suggest types of resources that will help your students do their projects. Marge Hagerty (page 17) offers suggestions to prepare librarians for the science fair season.

7. How can parents avoid offering too much help—or too little?

This is a common question and a big problem to which there is no easy solution. Some parents, in their desire to have their children do well in the competition, complete much of the project themselves. However, parents can play a more acceptable role if they limit their participation to guidance and support. Be sure to let parents know how they can assist by meeting with them or sending a letter home. See Linda Hamrick and Harold Harty (page 46) for a suggested letter to parents and see Stephen Henderson (page 48) for a story that suggests a positive side of (grand)-parental involvement.

8. Students sometimes have a hard time using measurements accurately. How can I help them?

Unless they have specific directions, students often express measurements in qualitative terms. For example, they will say the plant got "bigger." Encourage your students to make quantitative observations—that is, to use numbers in measurements whenever possible. Encourage them, too, to use the metric system in making their measurements—all scientists do.

9. How can I ensure that projects are safe?

This is a very important matter. First read the guidelines on safety in science classrooms prepared by NSTA (1978, 1985). Then, establish safety guidelines for your students, and be sure their projects and procedures conform to these guidelines. Inform parents, too, of safety measures.

10. Can my students participate in state and national competitions?

Many states offer both regional and state science expositions. Other competitions, scholarship programs, talent searches, and awards are also available locally and nationally.

11. How should I plan my science fair?

Planning a science fair requires much time and effort. Take some advice from those who have experience organizing fairs. See Brian E. Hanson (page 14); Deborah C. Fort (page 10); Ruth Bombaugh (page 18).

Barry A. VanDeman is educational services coordinator at the Museum of Science and Industry, Chicago, and President of the Council for Elementary Science International; Philip C. Parfitt is education associate at the Museum of Science and Industry. Photograph by Barry VanDeman.

Further Science Fair Resources

Aldridge, Bill G., and Johnston, Karen L. (1984). Trends and issues in science education. In R. W. Bybee, J. Carlsen, and A. J. McCormack, (Eds.), *1984 NSTA yearbook: Redesigning science and technology education* (pp.31–44). Washington, DC: NSTA.

Loiry, William S. (1983). *Winning with science.* Sarasota, FL: Loiry Publishing House.

Rice, Jeannie Rae. (1983, January). A special science fair: LD children learn what they can do. *S&C, 20*(4), 15–16.

Safety in the elementary classroom. (1978). Washington, DC: NSTA.

Safety in the secondary classroom. (1985). Washington, DC: NSTA.

VanDeman, Barry A., and McDonald, Ed. (1980). Nuts and bolts science fair blueprint poster. Harwood Heights, IL: The Science Man Press.

Youden, W. J. (1985). *Experimentation and measurement.* Washington, DC: NSTA.

The following science trade books might also be useful to your students as they prepare their science fair projects.

Beller, Joel. (1982). *So you want to do a science project!* New York: Arco Publishing.

Gutnik, Martin J. (1980). *How to do a science project and report.* New York: Franklin Watts.

Moorman, Thomas. (1975). *How to make your science project scientific.* New York: Atheneum.

Smith, Norman F. (1982). *How fast do your oysters grow?* New York: Julian Messner.

Stepp, Ann. (1966). *Setting up a science project.* Englewood Cliffs, NJ: Prentice-Hall.

VanDeman, Barry A., and McDonald, Ed. (1980). *Nuts and bolts: A matter of fact guide to science fair projects.* Harwood Heights, IL: The Science Man Press.

Webster, David. (1974). *How to do a science project.* New York: Franklin Watts.

Planning Ahead

A successful science fair takes plenty of time and energy—and organizing skills. Long-term planning and continued work throughout the year will help you overcome one of the biggest obstacles—finding time to take care of all of the details that add up. Start with a science fair master schedule that will help you find the time to reserve the space, pick judges, line up parent volunteers, prepare students, alert the media, and give it your all!

Getting a
on

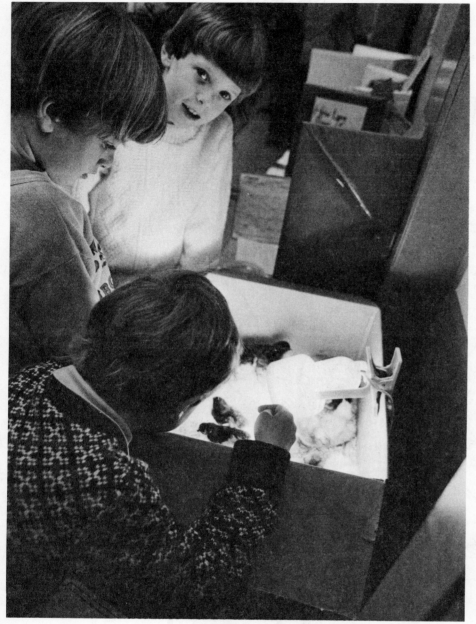

—William Mills, courtesy of Montgomery Co. Public Schools, Md.

——————— Deborah C. Fort ———————

The projects—116 of them in a public elementary school with 350 students—ranged from a test of the amount of dye in candy to a comparative study (by sex) of responses to breakdancing.

The principal, a former engineering and math major herself, required projects from the 50 graduating sixth graders. But the success of the annual Murch Science Fair in Washington, D.C., had to do with much more than administrative mandates. The science teacher and

the enrichment teacher, both veterans of 17 years of elementary school teaching—and of many science fairs—offered invaluable assistance to all interested contestants. And several parent volunteers planned carefully, pitched in early, worked hard and faithfully, and stayed long hours.

Plan Ahead

If you're interested in avoiding last minute starts and finishes on science fair projects, if you want to witness the death of the artificial two-week (or even one-night) project, if you even

dream—as the Murch principal does—of seeing a first grade project extend into second and third grade and beyond, get started now.

The first task of volunteers and staff alike was to help students struggle with the thorny problem of what, exactly, a science project is. Young children need some clear guidelines on scientific method, because the difference between a science and an art project can be something of a mystery to a kindergartner. Children in the lower grades can be taught to see science projects as opportunities for problem solving, for critical and analytical thinking, and for understanding cause and effect. Upper elementary students can sharpen research skills and discover new ways of conducting experiments.

Many educators believe that science fair projects should be part of the regular curriculum. Whether or not this is possible in your school, some fall preparation and continued work over the year before the big push in the spring will help you avoid some of the pitfalls that can diminish the value of science fairs or even make them harmful.

If a science fair project is an overall requirement, as it was for the Murch sixth graders, the science teacher—ideally in tandem with classroom instructors, volunteers, and the principal—should meet in the fall with all the children to give them an outline of scientific method, to define the categories in which they might work, and to try to get them thinking about their special interests.

If the science fair is a voluntary affair, as it was for the younger Murch students, divide interested children by age (say, first through third graders and fourth through fifth), and begin small group discussions, like those offered by the enrichment teacher at Murch, as

Jump the Science Fair

early in the year as possible. Because you will be approaching each child's project as a unique expression of his needs or her experiences, expect this procedure to take several meetings. Once the school staff has a sense of which children are interested in entering, provide volunteers with a list of their names. An early call to the parents of participants is likely to produce more help later, better sustained efforts on the parts of their own sons and daughters, and perhaps even some assistance for entrants who don't have strong support at home.

"I Can't Think of Anything"

The Murch science teacher finds that requiring her students each month to read part of any science magazine such as *Science News*, *Science Digest*, *Smithsonian*, *Ranger Rick*, *National Geographic World*, *Discover*, or *Scientific American* can help to focus students who think they have no ideas for projects. She couples weekly encouragement for all students with trips to the library as a counter to this kind of vagueness.

If a child expresses no specific interest but is tending toward something unfocused like "animals," encourage him to be more concrete. Does he want to know more about dogs, or does he want to learn about other animals? Does he have a dog? What kind? What exactly would he like to know about his uncle's Hungarian sheepdog that he doesn't know now?

Know Thyself

The best science fair projects grow out of something important in the child's life. For example, one Murch eight year old, the owner of a mixed breed collie and German shepherd, studied the responses of various neighborhood dogs to recorded wolf howls. A second grader

who had suffered a stroke as an infant studied his own ability to exert self-control through biofeedback.

Science fair projects should be in progress certainly by this month, ideally by last summer or even earlier. They should stimulate children to more ambitious future projects. In addition, most projects should involve mathematical skills; they should encourage organizational ability; and they should show children how to demonstrate method and results. However, not all science fair projects need be experiments calling for hypotheses and conclusions. Children can also learn a great deal from nonexperimental projects like those suggested by Margaret McNay on pages 30–31 of this book.

According to the Murch principal, what begins as a part-time effort should eventually be refined or expanded so that a project started one year can carry over into another year—and beyond. Teachers can encourage the choice of and commitment to longitudinal studies in topics like human growth and development (children can study themselves), methods of energy saving, changing purification systems, and conservation projects (what begins as an experiment involving plants can become part of a school garden).

"The Matthew Effect"

Like a strong science program, a science fair must serve all students—not just those lucky enough to come from homes where science is valued and practiced. Otherwise, we run the risk of further hurting children who already suffer from disadvantaged home environments—of intensifying what R. K. Merton has called, "The Matthew Effect." The words of the parable— "whosoever hath, to him shall be given, and he shall have more abundance: but

whosoever hath not, from him shall be taken away even that he hath" (Matthew 13: 12)—whatever their meaning in Christian theology, should not be an apt description for our children, particularly those who are not lucky enough to have parents who support them academically. Such children, more than the offspring of the privileged, need superior teachers as well as contact with peer academic achievers.

The Biggest Show in Town

In the best of all possible worlds, each elementary school student would do a year-long project. The Murch science teacher believes that she should help all children who want to enter rather than helping only a few intensively. Although the latter method does seem to produce winners, it is often hard to tell where the child stopped and the professional started. In addition, this approach focuses too much on winning and can deprive the majority of children of the chance to participate (or at least to do so without expert help). Parents and other volunteers *can* offer valuable help, but understanding the appropriate limits of that assistance is very important. Written explanations of who did what, like that offered by the grandfather of one young solar engineer, offer a possible solution to an old dilemma.

If you agree that the biggest science fair is the best, you should think about logistics now. Line up parent volunteers this month, for example, unless you were so well organized as to have asked for them on the first volunteer sign-up sheets sent out last month. And, if you're in a school with many students and not much display space, maybe you'll want two science fairs—one for the lower grades and another for the upper ones. Careful planning now can lead to a fine show in the spring science fair.

Labors of Love

The parent organizers of the Murch fair included a child psychiatrist, an artist, and a U.S. government administrator, whose hours of help provided far more than elbow grease, scissors, paste, and lunch from a fast food restaurant on judgment day (though their contribution included these items). Concerned that the children not become confused that science fairs "are" science and that the fair offer genuine opportunities for learning, not just ones for last minute competitiveness, the parents combined their offers to carry and to set up heavy and complex projects with an equally important willingness to discuss and, at times, explain concepts to the children.

Parental helpers stressed the need for children—their commitment, their time, their imagination. About a third of the students offered projects in the following categories: behavioral science (23 projects), biology (25), botany (7), chemistry (6), Earth and space (8), environmental science (11), health and medicine (6), mathematics and computers (2), physics (28). As they set up their exhibits and stood beside their com-

After the judges had made their decisions, Murch students inspected classmates' projects.

Ideally, judges talk with each child and respond to oral input individually, allowing presenters to be proud and informative.

good lines of communication among faculty, administrators, and volunteers regarding practical matters like time tables, resources for assisting students with project assembly, and availability of materials. They planned a November letter to parents signed by the principal and science teacher as well as by them to explain the philosophy of the fair and to encourage participation. They backed this overture with approaches to the students in the once-a-week science classes and in follow-up calls to parents of interested children.

After working on projects at home over the winter holidays and into January, students were encouraged in mid-February to submit written summaries of their work to the science teacher for her input. The principal made the science teacher available to participants in each class one hour a week; the sixth graders, whose participation was required, got more specialized attention. Then, during the week before the fair, parental volunteers were available after school to help with lettering, pasting, and assembling, as well as encouraging and explaining.

Set-up day was the Saturday morning before the fair (the weekend hours guaranteed a good deal of volunteer help from working parents). After the projects were judged on Monday, every class had a chance to walk through the exhibit hall and inspect the projects. The principal also arranged for early morning and late afternoon hours, so that parents and other interested spectators who worked would be able to see the science fair exhibits.

But the most important contributors to the success of the fair were the

pleted projects, the children were glad to offer comments to the classmates and parents who came to ask questions and admire.

Here Come The Judges

Picking the judges—how many and with what qualifications—is a decision that is important to the success of your school's fair. If the judges are part of your school's community, their anonymity should be closely guarded. This precaution is, of course, unnecessary if the judges are chosen from outside.

When picking judges—and you should get as many as possible, preferably enough that each project can receive several evaluations before the results are averaged—try to find flexible scientists and educators who will be willing to respond to the projects as wholes and who will not lose sight of the creativity that may fuel an imperfectly presented project. Before the judging begins, present each judge with a set of the criteria students have followed in creating their projects.

Whatever your particular criteria, the judges should note the display, and, as relevant, the hypothesis, method, data collection, and conclusions as well as the level of understanding the student demonstrates through the display and in response to questions. Ideally, the judges should be able to talk with each child and respond to his or her oral input individually, offering each presenter time to be proud as well as informative.

Murch's judges, recruited by the science teacher and the parent volunteers, included a chemist from a local hospital, an educator from a neighboring state's

public school system, a military scientist, and a junior high science teacher.

There Go the Judges

Another judging possibility—albeit a heretical one—is to give all participants A's. At one recent fair, the only acceptable judgments were Superior, Outstanding, and Noteworthy. In any case, make sure that all contestants win something—a ribbon, a certificate, or a medal.

Or, even more of a violation of the American spirit of competition, dispense with judgment altogether. Making each child's science fair project part of the regular science curriculum would render public ratings unnecessary, and everyone—from the most advantaged student to the least—would have a chance to participate. Such a procedure would also help to separate the parental contributions from the children's.

Fair Enough?

Once the projects have gone back to homes and (unfortunately) sometimes to trash cans, try to keep the memory alive to fuel enthusiasm for next year's fair and for this year's achievements.

For instance, do a follow-up unit on a particularly impressive project. The

Murch enrichment teacher had her third graders create a book called *Hydrilla Monster* based on one child's project.

In addition, she asked some significant questions:

- Did you like your project? (yes or no)
- Did you find out everything you wanted to know about it? (yes or no)
- Would you like to continue learning about it? (yes or no)

Although the results were mixed on the first two questions, a resounding 90 percent responded affirmatively to the third question.

So, if your students react similarly, note that fact and encourage them to get started early next year on science fair projects that are logical extensions of the experiments they seem unwilling to abandon.

A science fair wrap-up is also a good occasion for catching the attention of those students who didn't participate this year and who may wish now they had. Encourage them to start thinking now about areas that could become a project for the future. Help them to picture themselves as part of the fair next year even though they missed out this time.

Deborah C. Fort is a teacher and editor who was also a parent volunteer at the 1985 Murch Spring Fair in Washington, D.C. Photographs by Susan Hunter Silverman.

Wilbur and Orville Started Out on the Ground

A judge at the Murch Fair commented on her search for creativity, imagination, and scientific method, which she defined as "a question leading to an answer (though not necessarily the one expected)."

One fifth grader's winning study of "Heart Music" fitted her definition. He attempted to measure the impact on the heart of different types of music as measured by an electrocardiogram (EKG), loaned by an obliging uncle who worked as a doctor at a local hospital. His subjects were his 34-year-old uncle (76.5 kg), his 30-year-old aunt (51.5 kg), and his 8-year-old brother (22.5 kg). After learning how to use the EKG machine from his uncle (who also assisted by hooking up the participants), the investigator first tested his subjects' hearts without music, then, as they listened to "Footloose" ("a fast rock and roll song"), a Mozart concerto (a "slow, calm, classical piece"), Frank Sinatra's rendition of "New York, New York" (a "medium-paced song with a strong beat"), and the Beatles' "I Want to Hold Your Hand" (a "calm rock and roll song").

The young scientist's hypothesis, the faster the music, the faster the heart will beat (and vice versa), was *not* supported by his data.

He concluded that he had ignored many variables. For instance, he realized that the readings could have been affected by what the subjects had eaten, by their physical condition, by the volume of the music, and by their emotions: "For example, my brother laughed the whole time he was tested," a fact that perhaps contributed to his wild EKG.

Science Triumphant

Some of the hypotheses at the Murch Fair were proved.

One third grader studied hydrilla, which he described as "a noxious weed taking over the Potomac" [river] and which his display asserted was "wanted dead or alive." Early in October, he and

his family went down to a dock in the Potomac to collect hydrilla samples. He put 0.070 g of hydrilla in each of 26 large mason jars also containing various concentrations of river water, salt, and mud. The experiment stank so foully that his mother removed it to the attic at Thanksgiving where it eventually cleared and stopped stinking. Over the Christmas holidays, the hydrilla seemed to die and decompose; however, when the experimenter brought it back downstairs in January, almost all of it came greenly and slimily back to life.

The hydrilla died permanently only in very salty concentrations; mostly its decomposition was followed by a total regeneration accompanied by tiny snails whose eggs must have been in the samples the student collected in the fall.

Washingtonians, especially ones who enjoy boating on the Potomac, are deeply concerned about the spread of hydrilla. They wonder how far upriver it will spread—this Murch scientist thinks he knows the answer. Look for the snails, and you'll later find the weed.

Last But Not Least

Inspired by Laura Ingalls Wilder's *Farmer Boy*, a second grader experimented with the best ways to preserve ice. According to Wilder's title character, ice blocks 20 inches square cut from frozen lakes and buried in sawdust "would not melt in the hottest summer weather. One at a time they would be dug out, and Mother would make ice-cream and lemonade and cold egg-nog."

The investigator measured the room temperature, gathered his materials, surrounded ice with various substances, and recorded the time when the ice first began to melt. He studied the insulating ability of aluminum, water, paper, dirt, sand, and sawdust. Like Wilder's farmers, he found that sawdust works best.

Finally, an artistic as well as scientific upperclassman studied "Breakin." His full-color exhibit featured a large illustration—a brown man twirling on one hand (gloved in fingerless mitts), blue pants and red sneakers reaching for the ceiling. The scientist was trying to discover whether boys would react to breakdancing more than girls, and his hypothesis was that males would be more responsive. He observed, music box in hand, on the playground for several days, finding "Few girls stopped playing, but most boys stopped playing and began to do [move] to the rhythm of the music . . . There were 11 boys who did a complete routine."

Planning a Fair with a Flair

— **Brian E. Hansen** —

Though a successful science fair requires an enormous amount of time and energy, the payoffs are impressive: students get excited, parents become involved, and school-community relations are improved as the community is invited to take part in making the fair a success. That, anyway, is what we found when Sugarland Elementary School in Sterling, Virginia, held a fair last spring. More than 40 student science projects were exhibited, along with classroom science work from each class and seven professional and commercial science displays. Over 400 children and adults attended the fair. Planning, of course, was the key to its success.

First Steps

Sugarland's Science Fair Committee consisted of five volunteers—three parents and two teachers—who had expressed an interest in the school's science program. The committee began holding monthly meetings in October, about five months before the March date set for the fair. Working backward from that date, they established a schedule that allowed them to complete preliminary planning in about three months. (The two additional months would allow students time to work on their projects.) They began work by drafting the rules for the competition, the entry form, lists of suggested topics, and a cover letter. The rules included the entry and project completion dates, size speci-

fications for the final display, and judging guidelines. An important part of the rules was a statement that distinguished between a scientific experiment and an encyclopedia report and encouraged students to stay away from the latter. The entry form asked that the student describe the hypothesis, methods, and equipment for the proposed project, and it also called for a parent's signature to indicate permission for the student to participate in the fair. Suggested topics were drawn from the students' science texts, with one list for first, second, and third grades and a second list for third, fourth, and fifth grades. When all the entries were in, the committee checked to make sure the forms were complete and the proposed projects practical and safe. (No bombs or erupting volcanoes, please.) Several students chose identical topics, but this caused no difficulty since the finished projects proved to be remarkably different.

On with the Projects

To make sure that students (rather than parents) did the projects, Sugarland's committee required that all work be done at school. To make this possible, they arranged to keep the cafeteria open after school two days a week for half an hour each day. A Science Fair Committee member and parent and teacher volunteers supervised the students and took attendance to find out which students needed reminding to work on their projects. (No matter what the hypothesis, if a student abandons his or her plants in the storage room for four weeks without water, they will die.) During the rest of the week the student projects were stored in an unused classroom. For the next science fair, the committee intends to add extra after-school work sessions during the crucial first and final weeks. It will also offer additional help for younger students. (One first grader cried when her project didn't work the way she thought it was supposed to.)

Getting the Word Out

The committee member in charge of publicity really had two jobs: he needed to stir up school enthusiasm, and he needed to let the community know about the fair. The school menu and the parent/teacher newsletter were useful in publicizing the fair and its entry deadline among students and their parents. The committee also aroused interest in the fair by sponsoring a school-wide contest to pick a cover design for the program. Extramural publicity was provided by local newspapers, which were contacted both when the fair was originally announced and again a few weeks before Fair Night, with information about the date, time, and place and an invitation to send photographer-reporters to cover the fair.

The Community Participates

Sugarland encouraged community involvement in the fair by inviting scientists and science-related businesses in the area to set up displays of their work and products.

Brian E. Hansen is an associate professor of English at the Loudoun Campus of Northern Virginia Community College, Sterling, and he served as secretary of the Sugarland Elementary School Science Fair Committee in 1981–82. Photograph by Ruth Larsen, Loudoun Times-Mirror. Artwork by Marilyn Kaufman.

Science Fair Checklist

_____ Recruit five to seven volunteers (teachers *and* parents) who have good organizational skills and an interest in science to serve on the Science Fair Committee.

_____ Set time and date of fair about five months after first committee meeting. (Clear date with principal.)

_____ Draft science fair rules (entry deadline, size limits for display, requirements for final report and log of observations, completion deadline, judging guidelines). Emphasize requirement that all work be done by students. Urge experiments rather than reports.

_____ Design entry form (name, project title, hypothesis, method, materials, places for student and parent signatures).

_____ Make up lists of suggested topics. Check with teachers, librarian, and science texts for ideas. Have separate lists for upper and lower grades.

_____ Draft cover letter from principal introducing fair and explaining rules and schedule of after-school work sessions.

_____ Design final report form (student number, project title, grade, hypothesis, method, summary of observations, conclusions). Don't leave space for student's name because projects are to be judged anonymously.

_____ Design judges' evaluation form (number and title of project by grade, boxes for scores in each category).

_____ Organize school-wide contest to select cover design for program.

_____ Ask teachers to save their students' classroom science work to display.

_____ Locate and reserve a vacant classroom where students can work on and store their projects. Projects need to be locked up between work sessions.

_____ Schedule parent and teacher volunteers to supervise the after-school work sessions.

_____ Publicize (1)application deadline, (2)science fair night, and, after the fair has taken place, (3) the winners.

_____ Find judges (high school and college science teachers, district science supervisors, professional scientists).

_____ Find commercial exhibitors and professional science demonstrators.

_____ Solicit prizes or contributions to buy prizes.

_____ Order ribbons and certificates for participating students. (Some companies will print the event and school's name on them.)

_____ Arrange buffet for judges and demonstrators who may work through dinner before the fair opens.

_____ Plan and type the science fair program.

_____ Plan arrangement of booths to allow plenty of room for spectators.

_____ After the fair is over, send thank-you notes to parent and teacher volunteers, judges, and demonstrators.

—William Mills, courtesy of Montgomery Co. Public Schools, Md.

(Here was an additional area in which parents were an important resource.) These contributions, which were a big success, included moon rocks and a model of the Space Shuttle provided by the National Aeronautics and Space Administration and the telephone company's laser equipment. Visitors could operate broadcast equipment from a television station or inspect a sound truck belonging to a radio station, examine home computers lent by a local business or a microscope and slides supplied by a medical laboratory technician.

Judging

Each class had a display of the science work that students had done during the year. These displays allowed students to take part in the fair in a noncompetitive way. It also drew additional parents on science fair night. Judging the more than 40 projects entered in competition was done by a nine-person panel selected by the Science Fair Committee and composed of college science teachers, scientists, and science supervisors in the school system. Parents of students in the school were not eligible to serve on the panel. The criteria used had been adapted from those of Science Fairs International,* and they were weighted to reward experimentation rather than mere neatness, as follows:

Creative ability	35
Scientific thought	35
Thoroughness	20
Neatness	10
	100

Each judge worked independently to evaluate all the projects for one or two grades, recording scores on a sheet listing project titles but not student names; and each project was evaluated by three or four judges. First and second prizes and honorable mentions in each grade were con-

ferred according to the total points awarded by judges, who based their evaluation on a student's table display, including the equipment used, final report (hypothesis, method, summary of observations, conclusions); log of observations; and, frequently, a posterboard explanation.

What About the Prizes?

The prizes were donated by local merchants or purchased with money from parent/teacher organization funds. (The committee tried to interest national chain stores in contributing prizes by contacting both their local outlets and their headquarters but had no luck.) First- and second-place winners were presented with a certificate and an award—for example, a globe, book, or scientific model. Those who earned honorable mention received a certificate and a pamphlet about the space program. Each entrant got a blue ribbon.

Last-minute Details

After lunch on the day of the fair, several volunteers and the Science Fair Committee chairman arranged the tables in the cafeteria. They grouped the tables for the competitive science projects by grade level in the center of the room and the ones for the classroom science work and the professional-commercial demonstrations around the walls. Right after school, students set up their science projects, and teachers brought in their classes' science work. The judges began evaluating the projects at 5 P.M. and the businessmen, technicians, and scientists setting up their displays at 5:30 P.M.. By 7 P.M., with the judging and preparations complete, everyone got a chance to eat a buffet dinner of sandwiches, salads, coffee, and soft drinks provided by the parent/teacher organization. The fair began at 7:30 P.M. with a ten-minute program consisting of thanks to the parents and teachers who had worked on the fair and the presenting of prizes and certificates to the winning students. Then, for the next hour and a half the Science Fair Committee got *their* prize—they watched 400 students and parents enjoy the fair.

*Write Science Service, National Science Fair International, 1719 N St., N.W., Washington, DC 20036.

Other Sources of Information

AIRPORTS

If your project deals with aeronautics, an airport is a logical place to locate information. Airports often employ meteorologists that may help with projects dealing with the weather.

ANIMAL HOSPITALS

Often, veterinarians are willing to help with science projects. If you request help, call several weeks in advance for an appointment.

BOTANICAL GARDENS

Plant specialists can be found at botanical gardens. Maybe your community has a Garden Club with members who know about plants.

COLLEGES AND UNIVERSITIES

Colleges and universities have more than one thing to offer. Their libraries will probably offer a wider selection of references than a local library. Scientists on the faculty may help you and even allow the use of their laboratory facilities.

GOVERNMENT AGENCIES

Government agencies are usually listed under "Federal," "State," and "Munincipal" categories in the telephone book.

The United States Government Printing Office is also an excellent resource. Send a letter indicating what topic area you are interested in and they will send a catalog of available books and pamphlets. The address is U. S. G. P. O., Superintendent of Documents, Washington, D.C. 20402

HOSPITALS

Many hospitals have an education department you can contact. Perhaps your physician, dentist, or eye doctor can also give you help.

INDUSTRIES

Major industries often have specialists who may be willing to help. Try locating them with the telephone book or magazine advertisements. When writing to corporations, include "Public Relations Department," in the addressing of the envelope and letter.

NATURE CENTERS

Naturalists at nature centers might be able to give information if your project involves natural environments and ecosystems. The Audubon Society can direct you to nature centers and evironmental centers throughout the United States.

TELEPHONE BOOKS

The Yellow Pages of a telephone book, will list names, addresses, and general product information. When calling anyone, remember to be polite. Give your name and tell exactly why you are calling.

ZOOS

Most major cities have zoos, and most have education departments or zoological societies that may be able to help. They may be able to arrange a meeting with an animal keeper or zoologist. A visit to the zoo may also help you decide on a topic.

Reprinted with permission from *Nuts and Bolts A Matter of Fact Gurde to Science Fair Projects* by Barry A. VanDeman and Ed McDonald, published by The Science Man Press, Harwood Heights, IL 60656.

The Library Can Help

To the young scientist preparing for a science fair, libraries offer a wealth of inspiration and information.

Here is a list of ways libraries can help with school science fairs; explore them with your librarian and principal.

Update your collection of science titles. Ask the librarian to show you the science shelves or shelf list. Then suggest, by subject or title, books and periodicals needed. Offer to help weed the collection of obsolete material. Just an hour of your expertise could make a difference.

Contribute to the library's vertical file of clippings and pamphlets on science subjects when you can. Suggest subjects for new files which could help students with science projects.

Does the library offer students help with scientific inquiry—with making projects scientific? Consider acquiring some good books and filmstrips on the scientific process.

Above all, be sure you know how to check out different media and equipment. Can you locate items by subject? Can your students?

• *Establish special circulation rules preceding the science fair.* To avoid chaos and allow ample access to useful materials, ask the librarian to set special circulation rules for the weeks prior to the fair. Books dealing with physical science experiments might be reserved for two-day checkout, one per student. Or, arrange these books on a work table in the library, not to be checked out at all before the fair.

• *Set special study schedules.* Just before the science fair, the library might reserve more time for independent study or for entire classes to research projects under their teacher's guidance. Ask parents to help during these times.

• *Offer an in-service library session for teachers.* Before introducing the science fair to students, arrange a library session for teachers. The librarian can review the range and location of science materials, show pictures or slides of past fair projects, and discuss library rules and processes.

• *Introduce or review library and study skills.* Students will be motivated to learn these skills when they need them to complete projects. Just before the students begin their research, review the use of the card catalog and media listing, emphasizing science reference book sections. Discuss the Dewey Decimal System—especially 500s and 600s (pure science and applied science).

• *Record projects in progress.* The librarian can list in a prominent place all the science projects in progress and the names of students working on each. The recognition could induce reluctant students to participate. List projects by general subject and Dewey Decimal numbers, e.g., *Projects on Magnetism 538.* The list will indicate when to stop restricted checkouts and order additional materials.

• *Correlate science and language arts.* As the science fair approaches, the librarian can arrange presentations to students to include materials related to science subjects. What better time for using nature poetry and haiku for example, than when students are working on nature experiments?

The librarian might invite students who are participating in the science fair to write short science fiction stories. Such activities offer a break from working on projects while building students' interest in science.

• *Offer science centers.* Set up science interest centers during the fair or before. Assign responsible students to help prepare these. Each center should present an investigation for students to perform, provide materials necessary for the job, and suggest means for evaluating results.

• *Display winning works.* Students learn more from others' projects if they have plenty of time to examine the experiments. So, after the fair, honor the winners by displaying their projects in the library media center.

—Marge Hagerty, Librarian
Chinn Elementary School
Kansas City, Missouri

MASTERING the SCIENCE FAIR

Do you feel overwhelmed by details at the very thought of a science fair? You don't have to. Use this master schedule as your checklist, and spread those tasks out over a year's time.

I've been perfecting this schedule for about ten years, so I know it works. I began to develop it because as a young teacher I was a lot like my seventh-grade students—long on energy and enthusiasm, but short on organizational skills. The details became unmanageable.

Even a seemingly innocuous detail like arranging space for the fair can cause big problems if it's not attended to far enough in advance. The first science fair I organized was elbow-to-elbow with 180 students packed into the cafeteria. Now I reserve the gym a full year ahead of time.

I start by going over the basketball schedule with the athletic director to make sure the gym is free, and my seventh graders aren't scheduled for an away game on the night I want. Next I explain to the gym teacher that we'll need to set up on the day of the fair, and offer to trade spaces with her for that one day. Finally, when I've gained the cooperation of both the athletic director and the physical education teacher, I go to the principal and make a building request in writing. I also reserve the cafeteria as a hospitality area for the evening of the fair. This gives parents a place to be while the judging is going on.

Preparations inside the classroom also begin a year in advance. Each spring, I visit the various sixth-grade classes to tell them about the science fair. This gives the students lots of time to start thinking about science projects. I bring some of my most successful seventh graders along to demonstrate their projects. I share our "brag book" of pictures, newspaper clippings, and other evidence of the recognition my students have won at district and state fairs. This introduction to the science fair stirs up enthusiasm and anticipation.

The next fall, I give the students experiences with hands-on labwork. They learn the scientific method by performing controlled experiments. The students practice for the fair by writing up several of their experiments as formal summaries, including question, hypothesis, materials, procedures, results in a chart or graph form, and a conclusion.

Early fall is also the time to draft a schedule specifying the minimal requirements for the science fair and setting a due date for each requirement. The six requirements are: (1) performance of an experiment with data collection, (2) a formal summary of the experiment, (3) a research report with bibliography, (4) a visual backdrop, (5) an oral presentation, and (6) attendance on the night of the fair.

Structure is vital to the success of the fair. The schedule of steps and due dates provides the solid framework middle school students need. A number of my "learning disabled" students have won high honors at district fairs thanks to the structure the ten-week student schedule gave them.

Communication between home and school is another vital element to planning a science fair. At the first parent/teacher conference, I give parents a copy of the schedule and a letter that fills in the details. Parents are consistently supportive when they know what will be expected of their children.

Students spend three of the total ten weeks deciding on a project. Choosing the right project is the most essential step of the whole process. I don't want any student to work on a project which is so undemanding he or she won't learn from it, but I also don't want projects so difficult that students are set up for failure. Most seventh graders have never had to make choices of this kind before, so they need patient guidance.

To be fair to the students, judging criteria are based on the requirements they have been asked to meet. I give copies of the judging sheets to students well in advance so they know how their projects will be rated. They will earn 45 of the 100 possible points just for meeting the basic requirements. Knowing this motivates them to keep on schedule. The remaining 55 are quality points which indicate how well they meet the requirements.

When science fair day finally arrives, I can relax and enjoy myself. It's like a wonderful party! Students are dressed up and on their best behavior. The gymnasium has a holiday air. I make sure that I am free to greet the judges, who are local professional people. I put a high premium on student/scientist interaction. I don't assign judges more than four to six projects each. Students spend a class period after the fair writing personal thank-you notes. As a result, judges are eager to keep coming back year after year.

After the school fair, the students designated to go to the district fair get together to further improve their projects. Again, structure and communication are essential, so I arrange a time after school for each student and a parent to meet with me, read the judges' comments, and draw up a contract for the tasks the student agrees to do as part of our school's science team. These tasks include preparing the oral presentation for videotaping and practicing it in front of the sixth-grade classes when I make my spring visits. This completes the yearly cycle which began the previous spring.

RUTH BOMBAUGH
Langston Middle School
Oberlin, Ohio

Master Schedule for Director of the Fair

During the School Year Previous to the Fair

Preparation Outside the Classroom

Reserve the gymnasium for the whole day of your fair. (Talk to athletic director, gym teacher, principal.)

Reserve the cafeteria as a hospitality center for the evening of your fair.

Urge fellow teachers to assign your prospective students a research report.

Plan the format of your fair with the other teachers who teach the same grade. Possible options include:
1) An Interdisciplinary Science Fair: all students do a science project but the library research is a social studies assignment, the backdrop is an art assignment, the graphs are a math assignment, etc.
2) An Academic Fair: all the teachers cooperate, and students may choose to do either a math, social studies, science, or language arts project.
3) A Science Fair only the science teacher oversees.

Preparation Inside the Classroom

Visit the science classes to tell all prospective students about the science fair.

Schedule the current science team to give presentations to the prospective students and display their finished products.

Help any interested students to design science fair projects which they can work on during the summer.

Before Students Start to Work on Their Science Fair Projects

Preparation Outside the Classroom

Prepare letter for parents which states requirements that students must meet.

Prepare week-by-week schedule for students telling what they should be working on and what deadlines they should meet.

Prepare judging sheets.

Prepare award certificates and order ribbons. (Any student calligraphers ?)

Reserve public library and school library time for students to be shown reference materials. Arrange to have reference materials in the classroom too.

Reserve space and time for awards assembly.

Preparation Inside the Classroom

Stress hands-on lab experiences with data collection in your science classes. This reinforces concepts and helps students learn the scientific method in a concrete manner.

Require students to write up their lab experiments in science fair form. Make sure they have all the parts of an experimental summary—question, hypothesis, materials, procedures, results in a chart or graph form, and a conclusion.

During Student Preparation of Science Fair

Preparation Outside the Classroom

Contact resource people when they are needed for assistance.

Two to three weeks before the fair, line up your judges. (Personal contact by telephone works best.)

Preparation Inside the Classroom

Give it your all!

Follow the week-by-week schedule, and anticipate students' need to learn new skills. Teach how to write bibliographies about a week before they're due.

In the Ten Days Leading Up to the Fair

Preparation Outside the Classroom

Arrange hospitality. (Your school secretary, principal and/or fellow teachers may be willing to be hosts. Could the home economics students bake cookies?)

Make up the judging assignments and group sheets for each judge.

Make up name tags for the judges.

Arrange to have a volunteer photographer.

Alert the media (newspapers, radio, local TV).

Set up the tables and a microphone the evening before the fair.

Preparation Inside the Classroom

Continue to follow the week-by-week schedule and DON'T PANIC. The Last-minute Lizzies will often do wonders when the time crunch is on!

Go over the judging sheets in class and have students fill out the tops: name, date, title, number of project.

On the Actual Day of the Fair

During the School Day

Have students set up their projects during the class periods.

Let other grades view the projects, with your students serving as hosts.

Remind students to dress well for the fair and to be polite.

During the Fair in the Evening

Be sure you have delegated as much responsibility as possible. This involves more people in the fair and leaves you free to trouble-shoot.

Greet your judges! (They are V.I.P.'s.)

Enjoy yourself!

After the Fair

Finishing Up Local Fair

Average the judges' scores.

Fill in names on award certificates and host awards assembly.

Write articles for the newspapers.

Have students write thank-you notes to judges.

Preparation for District Fair

Draw together a science team of student volunteers and meet with each parent and student to draw up a contract of responsibilities.

Help each student follow through on his/her contract.

Videotape the science team.

The What, Why, and How of Projects

A science project should begin with curiosity and foster wonder. The best projects stretch students' investigative skills: questioning the world, wondering how it works, and delighting in and coming to understand its mysteries. But most students have little or no experience in the art of doing science. Use this section to help your students come up with project ideas. You can teach students how to design and to carry out projects and to think like scientists.

Science Fairs? Why? Who?

—————— Evelyn Streng ——————

"What's good for high school science is good for elementary science!" Is it? The attention given to science fairs at the junior and senior high school level has led to interest in and emphasis on holding fairs at the elementary school level. This trend has led elementary educators to consider the value of their use.

Opinions differ—as indicated by varying practices of "to have or not to have." Those who have not reached a conclusion would do well to recognize that the elementary science fair should (a) consider the nature and development of the elementary school child, and (b) should involve projects that serve the highest objectives of science education.

Child Development

Studies suggest that the elementary child is curious, and that natural curiosity can be directed to scientific investigation. Joseph H. Kraus, a noted science fair coordinator says: "Beginning science interests peak at age 12, with age 10 now coming a close second. Better than 10 percent of the nationally recognized students are launched toward a scientific future before they even enter kindergarten."

Although some childhood interests flower early, it is important to recognize the differences in developmental patterns. Also, perhaps only a few pupils in a grade-school class may be science oriented. Some creative, talented children may not have the patience or persistence demanded by "scientific investigation."

A fair amount of guidance and direction for the child-investigator is necessary, for the extent to which an elementary pupil can independently develop a project is questionable. The following criteria are desirable when deciding if participation of children in a science fair is appropriate:

1. Only children with a genuine interest in a science project and the initiative to see it to completion without undue adult prodding should be expected to participate in a science fair. A science project should never be a requirement for a class or a necessity for a good grade in science.

2. Any judging of a science fair project or display should consist of helpful comments and suggestions rather than comparative ratings or prizes. If projects are shown in one place, the emphasis should be on the stimulus of shared interests rather than on competition between classes or schools.

Suitable Science Projects

Suitable science projects are those which increase and direct a child's interest and competency in science. Worthwhile projects are those which are *problem-centered* and in which the *process* is important—not those which center on showmanship or gadgetry. Some categories of appropriate problems for an elementary science fair are

1. *Observation of the environment.*
• What kinds of trees seem to grow best in our area?
• What living things may be found in a cubic foot of garden soil?
• How do some insects change as they "grow up"?

These are the simplest types of problems, involving a study of the surroundings to classify and organize what is there.

2. *Demonstration of a basic principle of science.*
• How does electricity travel?
• What causes erosion?
• How does a machine make work easier?

These are not really "research problems," for the answer is known at the start. Their value is in enabling the student to clearly explain a basic idea.

3. *Collecting and analyzing data.*
• What is the average October weather like in our town?
• What is the rate at which a pet drinks water?
• How does the number of seeds produced by different plants compare?
• Is there a relationship between the phases of the moon and the weather?

In this type of problem there is no manipulation of nature by the student, but there are directed and recorded quantitative observations. This is more specific than simple observation, which is merely descriptive. Computation of averages, ratios, and rates; and performance of other analytic processes will be part of this type of project.

4. *Controlled experimentation.*
• What is the effect of temperature on the activity of mealworms?
• What is the effect of the moon phase on the germination of seeds?
• What difference does the kind of wire make in the resistance of an electric circuit?

This is the most valuable type of problem from the viewpoint of understanding science. It involves the use of controls—situations identical except for the one variable under consideration. Quantitative aspects are surely implied. It is apparent that the "answers" to some problems (e.g., "What difference does the kind of wire make?") are known to scientists, but they will be unknown as far as the children are concerned.

It is quite possible that elementary children may come up with some original problems to which answers will *not* be found in the science text. In the execution of a project, children may make the valuable discovery that they do not have sufficient evidence for a valid conclusion. A science project which concludes: "This experiment does not show any relationship between A and B; more experiments are needed" may be as meaningful as one which comes to a remarkably demonstrable "answer."

Shall we have an elementary science fair? Only if careful consideration is given to the nature and the needs of students and to the objectives to be accomplished!

Evelyn Streng is an associate professor at Texas Lutheran College, Seguin.

Who Needs the Competitive Edge?

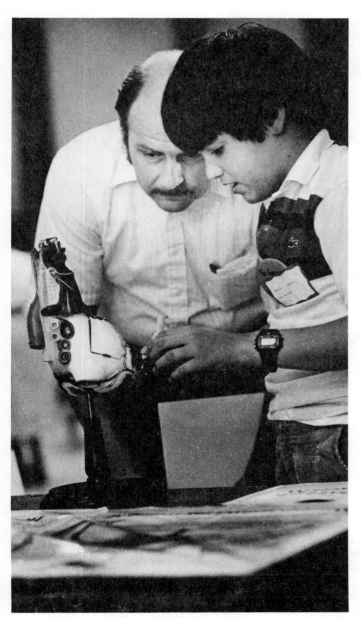

—William Mills, courtesy of Montgomery Co. Public Schools, Md.

— Bob Burtch —

Many science fairs are big, district-wide events and most are highly competitive. Such fairs can encourage and reward excellence, but they may not do much for students who are not particularly gifted—or competitive. The science fair at our school is designed as a teaching tool rather than a contest, and my aim is to involve and enrich *all* students in my fifth-grade class. Projects are judged on a 10-point scale by junior high school science and math teachers. The criteria include creativity, the quality of the display, and the student's ability to explain the principles involved to the judge. Although no prizes are awarded and an individual student's point score is not made public, I believe that our science fair achieves a number of important objectives. Here are some of the ones for which we strive:

1. **Create science awareness among the students.** Involving each student in a project which is to be on display generates far more interest in science than I, a single teacher, could ever do.

2. **Encourage parental involvement.** Many parents help their children with their projects. I invite this and ask only that, when the project is complete, students are able to explain what they have done.

3. **Remove the element of competition** I have seen elsewhere. Every student who participates in our fair receives a certificate with a gold seal bearing the school insignia.

4. **Interest the younger children in science.** Until this year when we outgrew our space, grades K–4 were able to visit the fair to see what the big kids did and to get a taste of science.

5. **Give students experience in sharing work they've done with others.** Students explain their projects in class, and many visit other classes to talk about their experiments and projects.

Our science fair has been going on for nine years now, and most people would agree that it's been fun. Many elementary school students have been turned on to science. (No one's ever been turned off because of losing.) Many parents have gotten involved. And this year we had to move to the junior high gym so we'd have enough room. What more could we ask?

Bob Burtch is a fifth-grade teacher at J.B. Nelson Elementary School, Batavia, Illinois. Photographs by the author.

Comments on a science fair without prizes, together with some prized topics.

—William Mills, courtesy of Montgomery Co. Public Schools, Md.

The Human Body
Teeth
The Digestive System
Tissue of Life
How the Heart Works
Blood
Can You See How You Hear?
The Anatomy of the Lungs
A Comparative Study of Bone Joints
The Kidney
How Does Exercise Affect the Heart?
The Human Eye
The Eye and Glasses: A Team for Better
  Vision
Orthodontia
Effects of Smoking
Drugs and You
The Human Body
Calcium, Iron, Vitamins A and C
Early Man

Animals and Plants
Flowers and Plants
Bacteria
Cheese
Sprouts
Herb Garden
Houseplants
Carnivorous Plants
Life Cycles of Plants and Animals
Bees
Dragonflies
Silk Moths
Seashells
Sharks and Teeth
Fish of Fox River
Amphibians
Frogs
Chameleons
Snakes
Dinosaurs

Birds
The Incredible Chicken
Beaver Lodge and Dam
Gerbil Training
Guinea Pigs
Horses

The Earth and the Universe
Crystals
Rocks, Minerals, and Their Uses
What is Inside Our Earth?
What Pollutes Our Water
Causes of Faulting
Volcanoes
Caves
Stalagmites
Glaciers Past and Present
Clouds
Local Weather
Weather—A Fact of Life

Involving each student in a project generates far more interest in science than an individual teacher could ever do.

—William Mills, courtesy of Montgomery Co. Public Schools, Md.

Effects of the Earth's Atmosphere
What Are the Effects of Air on Earth?
Sidereal and Solar Days
The World Beyond Us
The Moon
Planets
Stars and Planets
The Solar System
Why Do the Planets Rotate Around the Sun?

Physical Principles, Machines, and Technology
Simple Machines
Bridges
How a Canal Lock Works
Paper Recycling
Natural Dyeing of Wool
Conductors
How Electricity Works
Insulation
Good Conductors of Electricity
Electricity in a House
Electrical Circuits
Uses of the Electromagnet

Electrical Robot
Electric Motor
The Electric Cell
What is a Photoelectric Cell?
Telephones—Past and Present
The Telegraph
The Speaking Telegraph, or Telespacen
Transistorized Rain Detector
Electrostatics
How a Doorbell Works
Burglar Alarm
Five-way Radio Transmitter
Building a Two-transistor Diode Radio
Teaching Machines
Light
Optical Illusions
Reflections of Light from a Mirror
Color and Light
Grinding a Mirror for a Reflecting Telescope
Photography
Solar Energy
Solar Water Heater
What is a Solar Furnace?
Wind Power

Hydroelectric Power
Physical Properties of Fluids
Fractional Distillation
Ph Factors
Hydraulic Press
Two-cycle Engines
Four-cycle Engines
Atomic Energy
Model Rockets
How an Airship Flies
Airplane Simulation
Apollo II
The Apollo-Saturn V Program
Piggyback in Space
Hot Dog Cooker
LED Communicator
A Home-built Geiger Counter

Miscellaneous
The Loch Ness Monster
Chewing Gum
Graphology
IFO's, UFO's, and Astronomy
Pyramid Power
Inside and Out of a King's Tomb

"OH NO! A SCIENCE PROJECT!"

--------- Gail C. Foster ---------

Mention the words "science project" to a teacher, student, or parent, and you'll probably provoke reactions ranging from delight to aversion. More than one elementary science teacher has been confronted with wails of "Oh, no, a project!" when the assignment was introduced. And more than one (if he or she is honest) will admit to harboring occasional doubts about the value of doing science projects.

The problem may be that people involved in working with science projects sometimes forget what the projects are supposed to accomplish. The primary purpose is to encourage students to think critically and to investigate. A successful project has given its creator a chance to observe, infer, measure, identify, classify, hypothesize, experiment, manipulate variables, and interpret data. It has helped the student learn how to learn.

Guess What?

Science projects often cause difficulty because they appear out of nowhere, like a rabbit out of a hat. And children are supposed to be able to do a project just because the school is having a fair or because the teacher says that a certain percentage of their science grade depends on it. It's not that easy. Children may not have the process skills needed to do such a project. They lack extensive practice in observing and making inferences, and they may not even have participated in any simple group projects. Requiring a child to do an individual project without this experience is like introducing the alphabet and then expecting the child to write a novel.

Just Pick a Topic

Selecting a topic and identifying a problem are undoubtedly the most difficult parts of doing a science project. Common approaches include having children write down several "areas of interest" or pick topics from a list of time-honored favorites. If these methods don't work, children may be sent off to the library or media center, where they find "cookbook" experiments and then organize them into the form the teacher has specified. At best these approaches are artificial; at worst they cause children to work on topics in which they have no real interest.

A more productive approach is to introduce students—early in the school year—to the idea of asking questions about the world around them. Asking questions shouldn't be too hard, should it? Consider children's natural curiosity: "Why do balls bounce?" "What makes a radio work?" "Why are leaves green?" "What do spiders eat?" Unfortunately, as Lazer Goldberg notes, children seldom ask such questions at school, so you'll need to get them going.(1)* Set the stage for questioning by taking your class outside or gathering them around an aquarium, an insect zoo, or a learning center. A bulletin board with a new display could serve as a focus for questions. Talk about things you might have wondered about. Do ant lions turn into anything else? Will spiders eat dead insects? Does salt water boil as rapidly as fresh water? How does soap clean things? Will certain fish react to seeing themselves in a mirror?

Children respond quickly to this approach and begin contributing questions of their own. Explain that some questions can be answered by investigating while others cannot, and give some examples of both. Select some questions and have the children tell how they could find the answers. If time permits, groups could design simple investigations to answer simple

Looking At Objects Through Water

Insect Behavior

Gail C. Foster is a science teacher at the Energy Management Center, Port Richey, Florida. Artwork by Darshan Bigelson.

*See References.

questions. And be prepared for additional questions that arise from observation. For example, if children have experimented and found that they can lower the temperature of water by adding baking soda, they may have new questions that need answering: Will the water freeze if they continue to add baking soda? Will the temperature of hot water drop the same number of degrees as that of cold water? Will adding baking powder lower the temperature? How about yeast?

Creating Excitement

Once students are accustomed to posing their own questions, you can set the stage for selecting a topic and identifying a problem using the same approach you employed earlier to stimulate students' curiosity.

First, assess your class's attitude toward science projects. If students seem less than enthusiastic, blitz them with attention-capturing activities: try optical illusions, "eyeball benders," mystery boxes, mixtures and fluids, puzzles, tangrams, and magic tricks. Contests that pose problems with many possible solutions can be particularly stimulating. (Who can figure out the best method for floating an egg?) You can find suggestions for such contests or activities in Joe Abruscato and Jack Hassard's *The Whole Cosmos Catalog of Science Activities* (Santa Monica, Calif.: Goodyear Publishing Co., 1977).

You can also arouse curiosity by having students contribute to a classroom resource center. This resource center might include

- a mini-museum of interesting items such as shells, galls, lichens, seeds, magnets, magnifying glasses, a thermometer, batteries, wire, bulbs, a stethoscope, a tuning fork, balloons, candles, a funnel, a compass, pulleys, balls of various sizes, a gyroscope, a prism, a paper airplane, convex and concave lenses, marbles, a stopwatch
- a bulletin board with a word-and-picture collage depicting subjects that might spark ideas
- a display of advertisements for competing products and the containers the products come in to encourage comparisons
- interesting books and magazines like *Insects, Optical Illusions, Ranger Rick's Nature Magazine, National Geographic World, 3-2-1 Contact*
- lists of familiar places, people, and things that might inspire your students' investigations:

  personal interests—hobbies, pets, or leisure-time activities

  home—under the sink; in the refrigerator, pantry, garage, or yard

  neighborhood—school grounds, parks, vacant lots

  stores—grocery stores, drugstores, bookstores, malls

  people—family, friends, classmates

  media—television, movies, radio, newspapers, books, magazines.

Help for the Perplexed

In spite of all this, some children will need additional suggestions. Help them arrive at topics by staging brainstorming sessions, where class members contribute ideas and post the results for pondering. Or organize a Student Advisory Committee for Perplexed Individuals.

If a few children are *still* without a problem to investigate, you can fall back on teacher-child conferences, lists of specific projects, or a collection of experiments.

What Now?

When a child is ready to state the problem for the science project, he or she needs a brief conference with the teacher. In most cases you only need to help the child narrow the problem to a question that can be answered by experimentation. Let the child tell you what he wants to find out. You may need to help him simplify or reword the problem, but resist the impulse to tell the child what he wants to know. Simply ask: "What do you want to know?" and "How will you find out?"

Before beginning an experiment, the child should be able to express exactly what he is trying to find out (the problem) and how he plans to find out (the method of investigation). Theoretically, the child should find out as much as possible about the problem through observation and research. However, if the child actually researched the problem thoroughly, there would be few investigations because most answers to simple questions can be found in books. For an elementary school child, then, research should be highly specific and brief. (One side of one page will suffice for most projects.) Sources may include audiovisual materials, interviews, and brochures, as well as encyclopedias and magazines.

Table Talk

When your students are about ready to settle on their topics, use the chart above to give them practice in narrowing broad topics to specific problem statements and verifiable hypotheses. Work through the first four topics on the chart with the whole class. After each problem statement, ask students to design a simple experiment that would answer the question.

By the time you have presented the fifth topic, students should be able to

Trying Things Out

With a little practice, your students can become accustomed to locating topics, posing questions, and formulating hypotheses. Discuss the first four examples below as a class. Then, have students work together to fill in the blank columns in the last six items.

Topic	Problem Statement	Hypothesis
1. Conserving water	Do showers take less water than tub baths?	Showers take more water than tub baths.
2. Heating things	Do thick liquids boil as fast as thin liquids?	The thinner the liquid, the faster it will boil.
3. Balls that bounce	Will more air make a basketball bounce higher?	If air is added to a basketball, then it will bounce higher.
4. Ant lions	Do ant lions only eat ants?	If a worm or small insect other than an ant is dropped into an ant lion's hole, the ant lion will eat it.
5. Vision	Does eye color have an effect on pupil dilation?	
6. Rusting		Iron nails rust more quickly in salt water than in fresh water.
7. Soil	Does water soak into some kinds of soil faster than others?	
8. Plants		
9. Solar heat and color		
10. Hearing		

proceed with the rest of the chart individually or in pairs. After students have completed the chart, present them with a blank chart and ask them to fill in the whole thing. (They might do this individually, in pairs, or as a group.) Stress simplification. The simpler (and therefore more manageable) the problem statement and hypothesis, the less difficulty the student will have completing the project.

A successful science project should begin with wonder and foster wonder. As Cornell professor Verne Rockcastle says, "After all, science is not a subject; it is a way of looking at the world around us. Good science teaching helps children develop ways of finding out what makes things happen, and what will happen if . . . ."(2)

References

1. Goldberg, Lazer. "I Know the Answer, But What's the Question?" *Science and Children* 11:8–11, February 1979.
2. Rockcastle, Verne N. *Some Basic Philosophy of Good Science Teaching in Elementary Schools*. Atlanta: Addison-Wesley Publishing Company, n.d.

Resources

Cornell, Elizabeth A. "Science Fair Projects: Teaching Science or Something Else." *Current: The Journal of Marine Education* 3:17–19, Fall 1981.

Shephardson, Richard B. "Simple Inquiry Games." *Science and Children* 15:34–36, October 1977.

Smith, Norman F. "Why Science Fairs Don't Exhibit the Goals of Science Teaching." *The Science Teacher* 47:22–24, January 1980.

Ukens, Leon. "Inquiry with Toys." *Science and Children* 15:20, October 1977.

SCIENTIFIC INVESTIGATIONS

———Stephen C. Blume———

The fundamental purpose of children's science fair projects is to develop critical thinking that can be applied not only to science but also to other subject areas including, ultimately, reality. The best projects stretch the students' investigative skills furthest.

The elementary school science teacher can foster children's exploratory techniques by training them to use the scientific method in the creation of their science fair projects. Although this method asks that investigators (1) state problems, (2) list required materials, (3) outline procedures, (4) formulate hypotheses, (5) record observations, (6) analyze data, and (7) draw conclusions, elementary school teachers can simplify the process by having young scientists ask these six questions:

- What do I want to find out?
- What materials do I need?
- What should I do with the materials?
- What should happen?
- What did happen?
- Did I find out what I wanted to know?

Following these steps, students formulate questions their projects will help answer, perform investigations, and collect and analyze data to arrive at a conclusion or new understandings.

Lists of science project topics or problem statements of experiments are of limited assistance to science teachers. Resources are as near as the indexes of science texts and instructors' guides, to say nothing of the comprehensive creativity of children. However, problem statement frameworks can help the science teacher and the students begin. For instance, students can move from problem to hypothesis following the suggestions in the box below.

Projects that involve students in critical thinking and science process skills are best. I believe that show-and-tell displays of hobbies or models, laboratory demonstrations from science textbooks, or report-and-poster displays based on scientific literature are usually less valuable learning experiences because such efforts don't reflect science teaching's primary goals—developing critical thinking and investigative skills.

Stephen C. Blume is an elementary science curriculum specialist for the St. Tammany Parish School Board in Slidell, Louisiana.

Moving From Problem to Hypothesis

1. What is the effect of _____ on _____?

detergent	germination of seeds
eye color	pupil dilation
light	growth of plants
temperature	the volume of air
oil	the growth of beans

2. How/to what extent does the _____ affect _____?

length of a vibrating body	sound
color of light	the growth of plants
humidity	the growth of fungi
color of a material	its absorbtion of heat
vicosity of a liquid	its boiling point

3. Which/what _____ [verb] _____?

paper towel	is	most absorbent
foods	do	mealworms prefer
detergent	makes	the most bubbles
paper towel	is	strongest
peanut butter	tastes	the best

Margaret McNay

I once asked a biologist—an international authority in marine invertebrate embryology—about his childhood experiences with science. In particular, I wanted to know whether he had ever competed in a science fair. Yes, he told me, at age 14 he had entered his school's science fair. Fascinated by the living things he could see through a microscope in a drop of pond water, he had taught himself how to take pictures of them and had then made a display of his photomicrographs.

He did not win.

Some of us are not surprised: science fair projects are supposed to be experimental, to demonstrate that the young scientist can formulate and test a hypothesis, gather data, interpret results, and draw conclusions. Fair projects that display information or demonstrate a principle or process have often been considered insufficiently scientific and have even been described as not only missing the essence of science but also being inconsistent with the goals of teaching science. Such narrow-mindedness arises from a popular but inadequate view of the nature of science. Indeed, nonexperimental projects can evoke the spirit and nature of science as fully as investigative ones.

Some fairs are breaking with tradition by accepting entries from both categories, according nonexperimental projects separate status and judging them against separate criteria. For the sake of grade school entrants in particular, science fair organizers should embrace this practice enthusiastically. They should not ask the following question (with its implied negative answer) about a display that offers no hypothesis . . .

Margaret McNay is an assistant professor in the Department of Early Education, The University of Alberta, Edmonton, Alberta, Canada. Photograph by Susan Hunter Silverman.

—William Mills, courtesy of Montgomery Co. Public Schools, Md.

THE NEED TO EXPLORE: NONEXPERIMENTAL SCIENCE FAIR PROJECTS

"Interesting, But Is It Science?"

Instead, organizers could often answer in the affirmative, if they could agree that method alone does not define science. As useful as the scientific method and experimental design are, they do not define the limits of science. Popular opinion and the emphasis of many curriculum guides notwithstanding, science is much more than observing, hypothesizing, measuring, predicting, testing, and concluding. Essentially, science means questioning the world, wondering how it works, and, while delighting in its mysteries, raising hope about the possibility of coming to understand some of them. "What science has to teach us," wrote Jacob Bronowski, "is not its techniques but its spirit: the irresistible need to explore." Techniques are valuable only insofar as they make it possible for us to pursue something that has already aroused our curiosity. When we press children to choose a hypothesis to test or a question to resolve experimentally, unless we are careful, we may emphasize problem solving, measuring, controlling, and predicting at the expense of curiosity and intellectual involvement. Going too quickly and directly to the choosing and testing of hypotheses can bypass the wonder and delight in which science begins and can even deny children the essential experience of science.

Wondering and Questioning

Nonexperimental science fair projects offer children an opportunity to get involved with topics that sincerely interest them, even if those topics have already received a great deal of sophisticated exploration. Free from the necessity of limiting their investigation to a single aspect that can be tested experimentally, children can explore broadly and deeply, to the satisfaction of their own curiosity.

When will they learn experimental techniques? When a question arises calling for such techniques, there will be time enough to master them. And unless wondering and questioning are encouraged as fundamental scientific processes, children won't need experimental techniques anyway: they will develop no deep interests and no abiding curiosity about the world, and they will, therefore, have no questions to ask.

Nonexperimental Approaches

Some of the following approaches can help create an interest in science as profound as that of the marine biologist whose commitment survived losing the science fair prize 30 years earlier. Your students may choose to stick with nonexperimental projects or they may decide to change to an investigative mode. They may also want to combine their approaches. You can help them to learn that science offers an exciting universe enormous enough to accommodate inventors, observers, philosophers, describers, experimenters, and more. Help their horizons widen through encouraging them to work on projects such as the following (partially adapted from Evelyn Streng, 1966):

1. Presenting three-dimensional displays, reports, and posters based on literature searches. Many topics in which children are interested do not lend themselves to direct observation but can teach through being represented in objects, models, and diagrams. For example, students can make models of

the universe
the structure of atoms and molecules
the ocean floor

2. Building working models or presenting technical demonstrations. Children can come to understand many scientific principles through learning about technology. For example, they can

make a home-built seismograph
or show how a rocket works
or explain how nylon is made

3. Demonstrating a basic scientific principle. Even if children already know the answers to a question when they start to work, explaining the principle involved and showing how processes occur deepen their understanding. For example, students can show

what causes wind and water currents
what causes erosion

how machines make work easier

4. Observing the environment. Studying questions like the following can involve the children in a study of their surroundings that leads them to begin to classify and organize what is there. For instance, they can learn

what lives in a drop of pond water
how some insects change as they grow
what kinds of webs different spiders make
how plants disperse their seeds

5. Collecting and analyzing data. In these problems, children do not manipulate variables but go beyond the descriptive to make and record observations and analyze data. They can find

how fast bean plants grow
how the number of seeds produced by different plants compare
how efficient are various pulley systems

The Joy of Learning

Nonexperimental projects do tend to dominate elementary school science fairs, but this fact is nothing to deplore. Though experimental designs with properly controlled variables and appropriately drawn conclusions are important, they are not inherently more valuable than the sense of wonder and enthusiasm for finding out about the world. Children need to learn experimental techniques, yes, but they also need to explore.

The marine biologist who didn't get a ribbon at 14 continues to do essentially nonexperimental science. While his current work is more sophisticated than his childhood photographs of pond water creatures, it is essentially similar in nature. His descriptive studies of the invertebrate larvae that live in water help biologists better understand the complex mysteries of cell differentiation and the development of organisms. Much of his work does not require experimental methods, yet it is accepted as significant research. Why shouldn't we also recognize nonexperimental projects at the science fair?

Often the best way to approach an unfamiliar concept is by way of a familiar one. So when I wanted to ease the third-through-sixth graders in my gifted science classes into using the scientific method, I began with the familiar notion of fairness. "What," I asked them, "makes an experiment a fair test?" And "How can we design and carry out such fair tests?"

To answer these questions, my students, who were grouped by grade level in small classes of 8 to 14, embarked on a series of five activities. They had already had practice in measuring, reading tables, making observations, and preparing reports. Now, they would use these skills in defining and carrying out experiments.

I encouraged much group discussion as the classes proceeded with the activities: students were free to air their opinions—and revise them—at every step. The safe atmosphere that permitted children to be open about what they thought was, I believed, essential to their working through the questions posed by the activi-

thicker than water" could involve harm to a living being if the blood had to come directly from the donor but would not if blood from a blood bank was specified.

After individual students had made their final—and well-considered—decisions, the entire group discussed and evaluated these choices and then turned each testable statement into a question: *Can* you teach an old dog new tricks? *Does* a stitch in time save nine?

Having identified the statements and made them into questions, students now had to decide on methods that would be appropriate for testing the questions. To do this they needed additional information, so I explained various kinds of tests that might be performed—surveys, literature searches, and laboratory experiments—and students discussed their applicability to the list of testable questions. After some discussion, students readily agreed that, while the question "Does warm water freeze faster than cold?" could be answered in a lab, it would be easier to look in a book for the answer to "Do

WHAT IS A FAIR TEST?
LESSONS IN PROBLEM SOLVING

ties. And by the time we had gotten to the final activity, which asked students to design and carry out a test on a question of their choice, everyone had a good grasp of what makes an experiment a fair test.

Activity 1. Testable Statements

The challenge in the first activity was to select statements that could be tested from a list of 25 (see box, page 34) and then to categorize the testable statements according to the kind of test that would be appropriate.

Before underlining testable statements and circling the ones that could be tested without causing harm to any live animal, group members discussed their ideas—and often changed them. For example, some students revised their opinions about the testability of Statement 9 ("Liver is good for you") when one group member flatly declared that liver made her sick.

Students also began to see that terms might have to be defined before they could decide on the testability of a statement. Testing "Blood is

BY MARILYN FOWLER CAIN

Too many cooks spoil the broth.

birds of a feather flock together?" than it would be to observe and report on birds in the out-of-doors.

Activity 2. Creating Testable Statements

After classifying testable questions according to which type of test would be most appropriate, students went on to discuss the questions that they believed could be tested with laboratory experiments. As they discussed, they discovered that some of the questions needed more thought and further refinement. For example, they saw that measuring whether "_____ (brand) is the *quicker* pick-er up-er" is not the same thing as measuring whether it is the *better* pick-er up-er, unless "quicker" has been defined in this way before beginning the experiment.

Each student began by making up ten questions that could be tested by a laboratory experiment. Some of the questions reflected students' familiarity with TV commercials: "How many licks does it take to get to the center of a _____ (brand) lollipop?" or "Does _____ (brand) detergent break the 'static barrier'?" Others simply indicated matters about which students were curious: "Does a helium balloon make a louder pop than a regular one?" or "Does mold grow faster on bread than it does on an orange?"

Next, the group discussed the proposed questions to determine whether they could actually be tested. Were the necessary procedures feasible and could the terms be adequately defined? For instance, to determine whether a detergent could break the "static barrier," a researcher would need to define the term. (What does a static barrier look like? How would the researcher know when it was present?) And after defining terms, students discussed possible tests and rejected the questions that apparently couldn't be tested.

Activity 3. Designing a Test

In this activity, the whole group discussed tests they might use to answer one of the questions that had been accepted, and they then designed an experimental plan. For instance, the class considering the question, "Does warm water freeze more quickly than cold?" realized they would have to define some terms before proceeding with the experiment: Does *frozen* mean frozen solid or just frozen at the top? What temperature is *warm*? What temperature is *cold*? And they would have to decide what materials would be needed to carry out the experiment.

Students also discovered that even a result that is carefully arrived at might have to be questioned or qualified. What, for instance, if warm water did meet the experimental definition of "freeze" sooner than cold water? Would that mean that warm water would always freeze

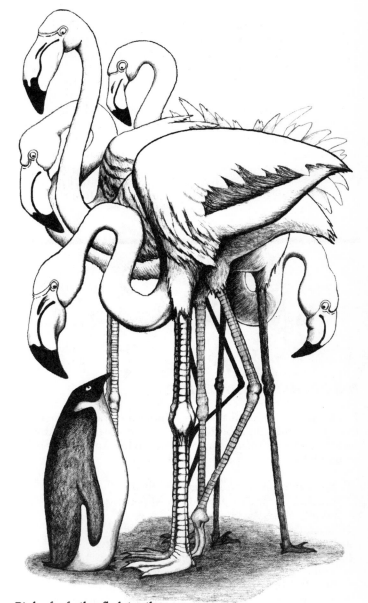

Birds of a feather flock together.

sooner than cold? Since *always* can be a long time, students were relieved to learn that they could qualify a conclusion—"Using my procedure and definition, I conclude that. . . ."

Activity 4. What Are Your Variables?

The issue raised at the end of Activity 3 led naturally to the idea of variables. Scientists need to be able to replicate each other's experiments both to check the accuracy of results and to build on them. But what if one experimenter puts the warm water in a deep freeze at 0° C while another puts it outside the laboratory door where the temperature is –10° C? Students were able to see that for an experiment to be the same for each experimenter—and a fair test—certain elements of the procedure would have to be the same, and I asked them to identify some more of the elements in the frozen water experiment. They came up with factors like the size of the container, the quantity of water, and the amount of time. When students had listed as many of these factors as they could think of, I underlined the crucial word in each ("size," "quantity," and "time") and introduced the term *variable*. Each of these underlined terms, I told the students, was a variable and would need to be considered if the experiment was to be a fair test.

Finally, I invited the group to think back over all the activities and attempt to define the term

FINDING TESTABLE STATEMENTS

Below are some familiar ideas. Underline the statements that you think could be tested; circle those that could be tested without causing harm to any living animal. (Some statements may be underlined *and* circled.)

1. You can catch a cold by being chilled.
2. "_____ (brand of paper towels) is the quicker pick-er up-er!"
3. "_____ (name of airlines) is ready when you are."
4. Warm water freezes faster than cold water.
5. You can't teach an old dog new tricks.
6. You catch more flies with honey than with vinegar.
7. Blood is thicker than water.
8. Sitting too close to a television can hurt your eyes.
9. Liver is good for you.
10. The grass is always greener on the other side of the fence.
11. Reading with only dim lighting can hurt your eyes.
12. Crossing your eyes will cause them to stay that way.
13. Birds of a feather flock together.
14. A stitch in time saves nine.
15. Too many cooks spoil the broth.
16. You can't stop progress.
17. A watched pot never boils.
18. A bird in the hand is worth two in the bush.
19. You can catch a bird by putting salt on its tail.
20. There is a calm before a storm.
21. An ounce of prevention is worth a pound of cure.
22. Cracking your knuckles will give you arthritis or make them larger.
23. An apple a day keeps the doctor away.
24. When the cat's away, the mice will play.
25. Rolling stones gather no moss.

fair. Proposed definitions differed, but all the valid ones included the following points:
• a question that can be tested
• definitions explaining the terms of the test
• a consideration of all the variables
• a conclusion based on the evidence provided by the experiment

Activity 5: Conducting A Fair Test

Finally, students were ready to design and carry out their own fair tests. Following the now-familiar steps, each selected a testable question and designed and carried out an experiment to test it.

The class presentations that were the climax of this activity made use of the experimental reports students had written and any samples they had gathered as they carried out their experiments. Using the group definition of a fair test, class members evaluated each experiment, and in cases where there was some question about the fairness of the experimental techniques—or the results—researchers had a chance to redo their experiments.

Fruits of Their Labor

Students did have a chance to enjoy the crown of scientific inquiry—publication—as the conclusions of each experiment were published in our newsletter. But seeing their names in print was only a small part of the benefit they got from these activities.

Of course what students gained depended to some extent on their age and maturity. But all of them developed a greater appreciation for and familiarity with the language of science, and they became more sensitive to the opportunities for applying scientific thinking and procedures in their everyday lives. (Some became enthusiastic analysts and critics of TV advertising, for example.) Students in the upper grades found it easier to think through the possibilities in designing an experiment than did third graders, and older students' discussions were generally more lively. But the third graders did become more aware of questions they might ask—and answer—and more likely to do original research— as opposed to looking in books—when science project time came around.

Oh, yes. The students' findings on the question, "Does warm water freeze more quickly than cold water?" can be summarized in one word: "sometimes." Students who defined "freeze" as freeze solid found that cold water froze faster than warm. Students who defined "freeze" as having a thin skin of ice on the top found that warm water froze first.

Marilyn Fowler Cain is a science teacher for the Office of Gifted Education, Austin (Texas) Independent School District. Artwork by Jim Ulrich.

Fair Evaluation

Science fairs should be valuable for everyone. If yours is not, why not reevaluate it? Do the projects exhibit the goals of science teaching? Do the judges use consistent and objective criteria? Are all students "winners?" Science fairs should not just be a time-worn tradition. They can be fun and challenging for all. Don't be afraid to evaluate or change the way you prepare for and judge your science fair.

Lawrence J. Bellipanni
Donald R. Cotten
Jan Marion Kirkwood

You have just hung up the telephone after a brief conversation with the science teacher at a local junior high school, and somewhere along the line you've "volunteered" to be a judge for the school's science fair. Suddenly you are responsible for evaluating projects that students may have spent months working on and for deciding which projects are best. Making these decisions is no easy task, but if you keep a few points in mind, you can turn your judging duties into a rewarding experience for both you and the students.

Regardless of the grade level you're working with, you should note the quality of the work the students have done and determine how well they understand their projects. The project should include research, experimentation, and application—not simply library work. But as you apply these standards, always consider the grade level of the student whose project you're judging and the general level of expectation for that particular fair.

Here are some specific criteria to use:

1. *Creative ability*. Has the student shown intelligence and imagination both in asking the question and arriving at the answer? Is the student original in deriving and applying data? Did he or she build or invent any equipment to use in the project?

Remember, anyone can spend some money, but it takes a creative person to devise the equipment needed for a particular project. Ask students where they got their ideas. Creative students are always coming up with new twists to old ideas; such ingenuity indicates that you're dealing with an interested young scientist. Collections may show diligence, but they seldom show creativity. So don't be tempted into giving them high marks unless they have some true scientific merit.

2. *Scientific thought*. Is the problem stated clearly and unambiguously? Did the student think through the problem and pursue his or her original question

without wandering? Was the experimental procedure well defined and did the student follow each step toward the expected outcome?

Did the student arrive at the data experimentally (as opposed to copying them out of a book)? Are the data relevant to the stated problem? Is the solution offered workable?

3. *Thoroughness.* A solid conclusion is based on many experiments, not a single one. Does the project test the main idea of the hypothesis? How complete are the data? How well did the student think through each step of the experiment? How much time did he or she spend on the project? There are few loopholes in a project that has been done thoroughly. Ask the student questions about the project to determine how well he or she understands the problem.

4. *Skill.* Since you don't know the students personally, you will need to have some way of determining how likely it is that they did the work themselves. Ask them if they had any help with their projects. (But use common sense here. If the project requires using an electric saw and the student is in third grade, it would

be permissible—indeed advisable—for an adult to perform this task.) You can usually tell how much of the actual work students have done by observing them while they demonstrate or explain the project.

5. *Clarity.* The project should be set up so that the judge can follow the procedure and understand the data without getting confused. Students should have written the data clearly, using their own words, and they should be able to discuss any portion of the project. The main purpose of the project is to show that students can formulate, test, and present research.

Though these five criteria are basic, the standards for judging particular science fairs may vary, depending on the grade level of the participants or the types of projects involved. The teacher supervising the science fair should make certain that each judge has a judging sheet, indicating not only the criteria to be used but the points that each item is worth. If you do not understand one of the criteria, ask the teacher or coordinating judge for clarification before judging begins. Your responsibility to the children is to be as fair and objective as possible, and that can happen only if all the judges use the same criteria in the same way. And remember: each child's project is very important to that student. So whether the project merits a blue ribbon or not, be sure to provide proper encouragement so that students will continue to investigate their own ideas.

Lawrence J. Bellipanni is an assistant professor of science education at the University of Southern Mississippi (Hattiesburg); Donald R. Cotten is an associate professor of science education at the same school; Jan Marion Kirkwood is a teacher in the Natchez (Mississippi) public schools. Artwork by Johanna Vogelsang.

Does Your Science Fair Do What It Should?

by Eugene L. Chiappetta and Barbara K. Foots

> *It's time to reevaluate our approach to these familiar research competitions.*

Every year thousands of students—bored, scared-to-death, excited, and confident—assemble their displays at science fairs across the nation. But why? Do they look forward to science fairs? Do our department chairpersons and district coordinators? Do we?

Science fairs can disappoint many students. After all, very few win prizes at the competitions. We ourselves often become frustrated when fairs demand too much energy and take away time we'd rather spend in front of our classrooms. Administrators feel overburdened when they have to organize facilities and solicit judges. But science fairs should be valuable for everyone. If yours is not, why not reevaluate it?

To be a success, a science fair must encourage students to ask the right questions—the whys and the hows. The following tips might be helpful:

• Encourage students to conduct science investigations that demonstrate the ability to ask the right questions and to find answers.

• Give students opportunities to collect data over an extended period of time and to analyze the data to determine the effect (or lack of effect) of a variable or procedure.

• Help students sharpen their inquiry skills beyond what is possible during classtime.

Many projects entered in science fairs do not emphasize investigation. Science fairs are often an incredible potpourri of

• models (volcanoes, animal organs, planetary systems, atoms) reproduced from pictures in printed materials

• hobbies or pet show-and-tells (horses, cars, leaves, arrowheads) that present information already available

• laboratory demonstrations (distillation, electrolysis, erosion, human pulse rates) that students have copied from a manual

• report-and-posters based on a review of books and magazine articles (birds, cats, trees, fossils, the universe)

Breeding Be
Insects for t
Organic Gar

• investigative projects that depend on critical thinking and science process skills ("What materials offer the best insulation?" "What characteristics of an airfoil generate the greatest amount of lift?" "What factors are necessary for a seed to germinate?").

Anti-emperialism

All of the projects listed above emphasize investigation, but to wildly varying degrees. So how objectively and fairly can someone evaluate them? It's the old "apples and oranges" dilemma. You cannot apply the same set of criteria to such different projects.

Furthermore, we do the model builders a disservice if we don't encourage them to go further than to reproduce a concept or an idea. Why not suggest that students include models as one aspect of an investigative project? For example, after a review of the

literature to determine the differences between normal and cancerous cells in various tissues, a student might build a series of models of both types of cells.

This example, you might object, is not really an investigation because the student has not collected and analyzed empirical data. Not all investigations, however, are empirical. Some of the most noted scientists based their theories on the research findings of others—Einstein was one. Recently, for example, we judged an outstanding middle school fair project on steroids. The project was an in-depth study on numerous aspects of steroids, including their use in athletics and cancer treatment. Although there was no empirical data, it was a great project.

Science fair projects should be an integral part of course requirements because they reinforce what students

learn in a good science program. Because fairs build inquiry skills, students are soon asking researchable questions, gathering information, and drawing their own conclusions. Science projects promote independent learning, encouraging students to pursue their own interests.

The five criteria

The criteria we use to judge science fairs need to address inquiry as well as individual effort. The first criterion is creativity. Focus on the uniqueness of the project. How worthwhile is the project, given the age, background, and ability of the student? Interview the student to find out whether he or she designed the project based on a personal interest or whether the project was suggested by a parent, teacher, or another adult. To what extent is the project an out-

—Marilyn Kaufman

Science fairs reinforce what students learn in a good science program. Because fairs build inquiry skills, students are soon asking researchable questions, gathering information, and drawing their own conclusions.

growth of the student's science course?

How much scientific thought did the student put into the project? Judges must determine the extent to which a student has taken in hand the investigative tools of science: observation, classification, inference, measurement, project design (control and variable), and others. Does the procedure fit the problem? A project on the effects of interferon cancer treatment would demand extensive research and careful organization. In contrast, a project on the effects of temperature on seed germination would require a carefully controlled experiment and the collection of accurate data over an extended period of time.

How well does the student understand the project? She or he should have read about the topic and be able to discuss data, concepts, and theories. The project should exemplify how a scientist conducts a research study. Students must be able to point out where in their investigations ideas

Eugene L. Chiappetta is an associate professor of education in the Department of Curriculum and Instruction at the University of Houston-University Park, Houston, TX 77004. Barbara K. Foots is an assistant director in the General Instructional Services Science Department of the Houston Independent School District, 3830 Richmond Ave., Houston, TX 77027.

are tentative and, in this way, realize the limitations of the data that they have gathered. Students must learn to avoid using the term *prove*. Science supports or refutes ideas, but it does not try to prove anything.

Consider the craft of a project. Students spend a great deal of time and effort in presenting what they have done. Give them credit for how well they display their work—neatness, organization, and visual appeal. Since youngsters often get help from their parents and other adults, try to determine how much others contributed so that you can reward a student for his or her own effort.

Finally, how well can students explain their investigation? Can they clearly communicate the problem, procedures, information gathered, and the conclusion both orally and in written form? How clearly does the project present the data and results?

The maximum number of points awarded in each of these five categories should reflect the purpose of a science fair. Generally, assess more points in the categories of creativity, scientific thought, and understanding than in workmanship and clarity. Be sure that judges and students know the criteria and the point system in advance.

Even with the best criteria, other problems can crop up. Be ready. Competition can sometimes detract from the goals of science fairs. Often parents get too involved because they want their children to win. By giving too much guidance and direction, they rob students of opportunities to develop their own creative abilities and to learn self-motivation. This also places students who do most of their own work at a disadvantage. Some school districts have even discontinued science fairs because parents were overinvolved in their children's science fair projects.

Plan it right

At times, school district fairs also put undue pressure on science teachers. Frequently, we must devote too much class time to these events. We often feel burdened with excessive paperwork and laboratory preparation in addition to our regular course instruction. Sometimes it seems that science fairs just add to the workload. The key to avoiding such problems is, of course, planning. A science fair committee of teachers and parents should establish a timetable and judging criteria, handle publicity, select awards, and explain what students are expected to do.

Establish early in the school year the purpose for the fair in your school and district so that students and teachers realize that projects should reflect the investigative aspect of science as well as the influence of science and technology in society. Arrange for students to work on projects throughout the school year so that the science fair will be a natural extension of your science course and the district's science program.

Science fairs should not be just a time-worn tradition. They can be fun and challenging for both students and teachers. But we must not be afraid to overhaul them, to make some real changes in the way we prepare for them and the way we judge them. These crazy-quilt displays of varied talent and effort should be a highlight of the academic year. ∎

INJECTING OBJECTIVITY INTO SCIENCE FAIR JUDGING

Use of a standard evaluation form reflecting specific criteria may help to clarify science fair goals for both students and judges.

Harvey Goodman

Many science fair evaluators have suffered at one time or another from the nagging feeling that judging is, at best, subjective and, at worst, borders on the arbitrary—a sad commentary in light of the tremendous amount of effort that students put into their projects.

A major part of the problem undoubtedly lies in the fact that we have not well defined the goals of science fairs, nor evaluated how these coincide with the broader goals of science teaching. Author Norman F. Smith (page 42) points out how few projects are investigative, involving students in critical thinking and science processes. Most awards, he observes still go to traditional "library research and poster" projects.

Another factor that may account for the subjectivity of the judging process is the lack of availability of objective criteria—criteria so designed that a judge evaluating a project in a specialty other than his own could arrive at a conclusion that is at least comparable with that of other members of the judging team.

Traditionally, judges are asked to evaluate students' projects according

[1] "Why Science Fairs Don't Exhibit the Goals of Science Teaching," by Norman F. Smith, *The Science Teacher* 47:22; January 1980.

Harvey Goodman is an assistant principal and supervisor in the biology department at Grover Cleveland High School, 2127 Himrod St., Ridgewood, NY 11385.

to a scheme that looks something like the following:

Creativity (30 points)
Logical Thought (25 points)
Thoroughness (10 points)
Skill (15 points)
Clarity of Presentation (15 points)

What is the likelihood that two judges using this scheme could arrive even approximately at the same point value for a project? How helpful are these criteria to a student planning a project? How is creativity to be evaluated?

Usually, when one evaluates a project, one has (or should have) some criteria of a different sort in mind. What one really is looking to see is, for example: whether the project really reflects the problem statement; whether the hypothesis arose from adequate background reading; whether the procedures used were appropriate for the problem; whether the observations were accurately recorded and appropriately displayed; whether the apparatus was appropriate for the experiment; and whether further research problems were suggested by the project.

How can one get judges to focus on these criteria (or whatever standards are decided on)? I would suggest that we begin by drawing up standard evaluation forms which reflect the values of each fair and which direct the evaluator's attention to specific elements of the project. The format might look something like the following:

Science Fair Project Evaluation Form

0 = Cannot make a judgment
1 = Poor
2 = Fair
3 = Satisfactory
4 = Good
5 = Excellent

Rank each of the following based on the rating system given above:

The problem was clearly stated. (*Problem formulation.*)

Appreciable time was evidently spent searching for and reading scientific articles. (*Background reading.*)

Background reading was appropriate both in quality and scope. (*Background reading.*)

The hypothesis was stated clearly and reflected the background readings. (*Hypothesis formation.*)

The experimental design demon-

strated understanding of the scientific method. (*Methodology.*)

Apparatus and equipment were appropriately designed and/or used. (*Materials.*)

Observations were clearly summarized. (*Observations.*)

Interpretation of data conformed with observations. (*Observation.*)

Tables, graphs, and illustrations were used effectively in interpreting data. (*Observation.*)

Conclusions and summary remarks were justified on the basis of experimental data. (*Conclusion.*)

The experiment was repeated several times to establish validity of results. (*Validity.*)

A log book was used to record experimental data, ideas, interpretations, and conclusions. (*Record keeping.*)

The bibliography contained a significant number of relevant and timely references. (*Background reading.*)

Limits of accuracy of measurements were stated. (*Measurement.*)

Work on the project suggested new problems for future research. (*Future research.*)

Oral presentation was made in the time allotted, with all phases of the project discussed. (*Interview.*)

The researcher answered questions effectively and accurately. (*Interview.*)

The oral presentation made good use of visual aids. (*Interview.*)

The student initiated his or her own research project. (*Initiative.*)

The display board was effective in presenting the project. (*Display board.*)

The maximum number of points that a candidate may obtain is 100 percent; awards may be granted in accordance with the following scores:

60 - 69—Honorable Mention
70 - 79—Third Prize
80 - 89—Second Prize
90 - 100—First Prize

In the event that a judging team consists of two or more members, the final score is the team average.

. . .

If the goals of each science fair were adequately described to judges, if judges were given evaluation forms reflecting specific criteria by which projects could be evaluated in a more objective way, we would all benefit— students, teachers, and judges. ∎

Why is it that models, posters, show-and-tell, and laboratory demonstrations are so predominant at science fairs, while projects dealing with discovery and investigation are decidedly scarce?

Norman F. Smith

Why Science Fairs Don't Exhibit the Goals of Science Teaching

One need attend only a few elementary- and intermediate-level science fairs to discover that they are all more or less alike. A second discovery will follow close behind: most of the projects in these fairs have little relevance to the goals of science teaching. From my long experience as a scientist, plus many assignments as a science-fair advisor and judge, I suggest that the cause of this situation lies where no one may have thought to look—in the way science fairs are operated and judged.

An analysis of the kinds of science-fair projects we see time after time at the elementary and intermediate levels clearly shows a disparity between the goals of science fairs and those of science teaching. Nearly all fair projects can be placed in one of the following five categories:

1. Model building (for example, the solar system, volcanoes, clay models of frog organs);

2. Hobby or pet show-and-tell (for example, arrowheads, slot cars, dogs, baby chicks);

3. Laboratory demonstrations right out of the textbook or laboratory manual (for example, distillation, electrolysis, seed germination);

Norman F. Smith is a mechanical engineer and a former NASA aerospace research scientist. He is the author of several science trade books for young people. (Address: North Hero, VT 05474.)

" . . . the first-in-class was awarded, for at least the thousandth time in the history of science fairs, to the students who crushed the cans with air pressure."

4. Report-and-poster projects from literature research (for example, fossils, birds, bees, the astronauts, the ear);

5. Investigative projects that involve the student in critical thinking and science processes, such as measuring, reducing data, and drawing conclusions (for example, tests of reaction time, effectiveness of various detergents, comparison of the performance of vacuum bottles with insulated jugs).

If the goal of science teaching is to improve skills in model building, library research, poster making, or following laboratory-manual directions, then projects from the first four categories are appropriate. Such projects may indeed stimulate students' interest in science and increase their knowledge of science, in addition to contributing to social and communication skills. But if one of the primary goals in science teaching is to teach critical thinking, inquiry, and investigative skills, then projects in the first four categories simply do not match this goal, or are, at best, ineffective approaches to it. The essence of science is found only in category 5, in which the student must conceive and plan a project, perform an investigation, and analyze data to arrive at some conclusions or some new understanding.

Problems worth investigating

This being the case, why is it that projects in the first four categories (models, posters, show-and-tell, and laboratory demonstrations) are predominant at science fairs, while projects dealing with discovery and investigation are decidedly scarce? This is a question long overdue for investigation; it applies as well to extra-credit projects and normal laboratory activities.

Discussing this question with science teachers yields a number of viewpoints. Some teachers blame the poor science backgrounds of those in their own profession, especially among elementary teachers. Because elementary teachers may be neither highly skilled in science, nor entirely certain about the goals of science teaching, they tend to be more comfortable with activity closely allied with bookwork. Students, too, are more comfortable with projects that can be lifted from books than with less familiar and more original projects that probe the unknown.

Other teachers point out that the kinds of projects currently popular represent a "point of entry" into science for the younger student. This viewpoint has validity, and some use of these kinds of projects is undoubtedly justified.

As it turns out, however, most students remain stuck with these projects year after year, repeating selections from the first four categories until they move into high school. Then the rules suddenly change, and only original experimental or technical projects generally are accepted, at least at major competitions. What are missing or at least underemphasized in the present system are *transition* projects, in which the student moves from the easy poster project to a deeper look at the science aspects of his topic, and finally to sampling the process of investigation. (Indeed, some of the exotic projects in high-school science fairs are more oriented to technology than to science; consequently, one wonders whether these students have *ever* had the experience of designing a simple experimental project.)

Many teachers are aware that the question of what kinds of projects might or should be done in science fairs is almost never discussed. In particular, there is little or no discussion or agreement beforehand among teachers, students, and science-fair judges as to the *purposes* of the endeavor and the *criteria* by which entries will be judged. As a result, teachers find themselves coaching students in the execution of projects that will be judged by persons unknown to them, and according to criteria that are not carefully considered by those making the rules.[1]

In my view, the most startling reason for the present emphasis on non-investigative projects is the orientation of the judges themselves, which causes them to reinforce projects in the first four categories and to discourage investigative projects. While this orientation may seem contrary to the interests and instincts of scientists, it is really quite understandable, given the usual conditions of scientists' involvement in science fairs.

View from the scientist

The lot of the scientist asked to judge a science fair is not a happy one. Armed with a specialty in some branch of science, but often with little or no knowledge of science *education*, he surveys, clipboard in hand, a scene that is quite foreign to his professional world—a vast arena of eager students of widely varying competencies, who are presiding over projects that vary even more widely in quality and science content. The casual observer may marvel at the diversity of projects he sees, but the judge has the grim job of sorting out these projects and finding some basis for declaring a few of them the "winners."

How "winners" are often chosen is best illustrated by true examples from a junior-high science fair. On one table the judge finds a project labeled "Air Pressure," with a Bunsen burner and three or four gallon cans that have been crushed by air pressure. There are also

---

[1] Judging criteria usually consist of items like: originality, thoroughness, accuracy, clarity, organization, neatness, creativity and skill, dramatic effect, technical skill and workmanship, social implications, communicative skills, science content, and scientific approach. Such criteria are usually vaguely defined for the judges, if at all, and are weighted very differently from one science fair to another. It is amazing that items such as "science content" and "scientific approach" are sometimes omitted or are weighted as little as 10 percent.

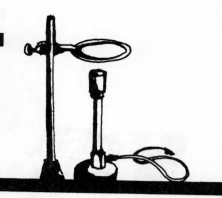

" . . . in the dazzle of textbook competence from the next booth, the spark of inquiry glowing among the eggshells was unnoticed by the scientist . . . "

two other gadgets right out of the lab manual neatly hung on ringstands so that people can blow into them to demonstrate "air pressure" for themselves. The posters are adequate; the students are responsive to the questions of the judge and impress him with their understanding of the topic.

A few tables away is a project in which two students have compared the ability of a thermos bottle, a plastic jug, and two or three other kinds of containers to keep liquids hot. They have described on posters their purpose and test procedures. Their equipment is on display, and other posters show tables of data and graphs of the variations of temperature with time that the students stayed up half the night to measure. The graphs are neatly made and the data, though a bit rough, look good. Under questioning, the students show that they have drawn some conclusions, but their understanding of the science principles behind what they have done seems somewhat shaky to the judge. He finds that they don't know a great deal about heat, how heat is transmitted, or about insulation.

As the reader by now has guessed, the first-in-class was awarded, for at least the thousandth time in the history of science fairs, to the students who crushed the cans with air pressure. Second and third awards went to excellent library-research-and-poster projects on fish and birds, respectively. The investigation of thermos bottles and insulated jugs did not place or receive any recognition.

The process by which the judge had arrived at his decision later became clear from discussions with him. With only general criteria to guide him and a sketchy, at best, understanding of children and science teaching, he had relied on his best instincts as a scientist. The questionable understanding of science principles shown by the thermos investigators troubled him—perhaps "repelled" would be a better word—and kept him from seriously considering their project, whereas he was drawn to-

ward the apparent competence shown in the demonstration-and-poster project. A "good" understanding of some concepts of air pressure and a "good" laboratory *demonstration* were more worthy, according to his standards, than a "fair" ability to conduct an *investigation* backed by only a "fair" understanding of the concepts involved.

But what could be wrong with that? We all know that competence is vital in science, don't we? And don't we also try to teach proper understanding of science concepts and principles?

"Investigation" rebuffed

The consequences of such decisions by science-fair judges, however, are obvious. The students who made earnest—and perhaps fruitful—attempts to explore the unknown with an investigative project have been rebuffed. If they try at all next year, they will probably seek a project along the safer lines of library research or laboratory demonstration in which they may, through book learning and practice, acquire the aura of competence for which the "system" has shown clear preference.

Lest anyone think this an isolated event, I cite two other projects from the same fair. One is a demonstration of refraction, well-executed by a pair of confident students. They know the principle of refraction and demonstrate it in half a dozen ways using a slide projector and an aquarium, along with several drawings. Their competence in this topic is impressive.

On the next table is a project on chickens and eggs, an interest the student brought from home. With some guidance from the teacher, the student undertook to measure the thickness of eggshells from different kinds of chickens. At first, she couldn't locate a micrometer, but did have a feeler gauge. She used an old automobile spark plug, gapping it by trial and error to fit each shell, then measuring the gap with the feeler gauge. Later she was able to locate a micrometer and used it to check and

refine her earlier measurements. Her display was unimpressive, her manner shy, but from her data one could learn about the range of thickness of eggshells, and—a most interesting item—the dimensional tolerance within which the chicken manufactures the shell. (Anybody out there know that?) She also showed a comparison between the thickness of a standard shell and a "soft-shell"—a defective egg occasionally laid by some chickens. She understood well the dietary deficiency that causes soft-shelled eggs and what to do about it.

But in the dazzle of textbook competence from the next booth, the spark of inquiry glowing among the eggshells was unnoticed by the scientist—indeed, may have been snuffed out by his lack of interest and his final decision. First place went to the demonstration of refraction, second place to the familiar "How Seeds Grow," and third place to the ever-popular "How The Ear Functions." Should the student who struggled with eggshells be brave enough to do another project on chickens—or any other topic—next year, she will put curiosity aside and generate instead the most elaborate library-research, poster, show-and-tell project she can muster. Who could blame her?

The dominance of non-investigative projects in today's science fairs suggests that fairs have drifted far from the avowed goals of science teaching. A fresh examination is needed to bring the goals of science fairs and science teaching back together.

Here's one modest proposal: if fair sponsors were to set up a separate judging category for investigative projects, they would immediately motivate students and teachers to move in this direction by guaranteeing recognition of such projects. Over a period of a few years the present monotonous fairs might begin to evolve into new "discovery fairs" in which students, teachers, and the public would discover the adventure of investigation and experience the true meaning of science. ∎

The Parents' Role

Undertaking a project for a science fair can be a daunting prospect for children, especially if they are expected to work without the teacher's constant guidance. A little preparation, however, can help a parent assume the role of a guide. This can be more than a learning experience; opportunity for sharing is enhanced when parent and child set out on the road of inquiry together.

SCIENCE FAIRS:
A Primer for Parents

This article is aimed at a group interested in the ins-and-outs science projects—parents. You might want to send this article, or a letter of your own, home with students the next time they are assigned a science project.

—— Linda Hamrick ——
Harold Harty

Odds are that sometime during your child's elementary or middle school years, he or she will be involved in some type of science fair project. And, if fair guidelines permit, you're probably going to be involved too. But don't panic, because you know more than you think you do. Common sense—and the recollection of your own experiences—tell you that doing the project over a reasonable period of time, instead of cramming it into one or two frantic nights, is essential to its success and your sanity. You also probably know that working on a project with your child can be a source of immense satisfaction to both of you.

Naturally, some questions about logistics remain, but we hope the guide-

Linda Hamrick is head of the science department at The Canterbury School, Fort Wayne, Indiana. Harold Harty is an associate professor of science education at Indiana University, Bloomington. Photograph by Charles R. Hamrick.

lines that follow will answer many of them.

Getting Acquainted with the Project

First, be sure you are familiar with any guidelines for the project that have been set by the teacher or fair committee. Usually this type of information is sent home as a bulletin to parents, and you might tape the bulletin to a wall or refrigerator door so it doesn't get lost.

Help your child to allow plenty of time to do the project. Begin at least four weeks before the deadline, and, if the school allows more time, take advantage of it. Try to set aside time every other day or so for work sessions.

It's a good idea to make the sessions fairly short (about 20 minutes). This will allow for slow but steady progress. It will also accommodate the limited attention span that children usually have and ensure that each encounter is pleasant rather than tiring.

Don't get hung up on details. Children often become very worried about small points, like choosing a paint color, and spend a disproportionate amount of time trying to make up their minds. Usually the decision is so hard to make because there is no right or wrong answer. On the other hand, if your child is puzzled about what seems to be an issue of substance or of size limita-

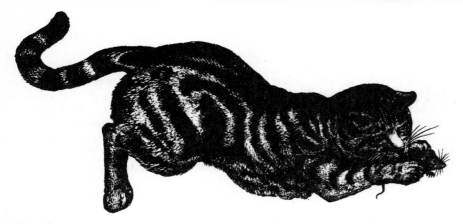

tions, for example, a quick call or note to the school can probably take care of things.

Scientific Approaches

Science projects, whether constructed for classroom display or for competition, share certain basic characteristics. This is the case because all seek to follow the scientific method in the way they approach a problem, and all make use of inductive reasoning.

Inductive reasoning is a tool used by scientists and means simply that the investigator bases conclusions on an examination of the data that he or she has gathered. A simple example would be an inductive investigation of whether mammal hairs are all alike or whether they differ from animal to animal. The inductive approach would require gathering hairs from mammals that were handy—family members, pets, cooperative friends—and looking at them with a microscope and perhaps drawing pictures of them before coming to a conclusion.

The scientific method involves four steps: forming a hypothesis, designing and describing the method of investigation, gathering and analyzing data, and drawing conclusions. The hypothesis is a statement that will either be proven or challenged. Teachers sometimes urge children to ask a question instead of stating a hypothesis, but answering a question does not always require scientific investigation. At any rate, by defining the purpose first, the child can see what information he or she must seek in order to draw conclusions.

Next comes the description of the method, a statement of how the investigation is to be carried out. It paves the way for the actual investigation and forces the child to think ahead of time about the investigative plan of attack. The information gathered during the investigation is called data. After the data are collected, they need to be tabulated or diagrammed to facilitate their analysis. From the data, the child will confirm or challenge the hypothesis or answer the question asked. Thus, the project comes full circle to the question that started the adventure.

Setting Up the Display

Once the project is completed, the next step is to set up a display to show the course of the investigation and explain its outcome. Three-panel displays are the most common, both because they are free-standing and because they accommodate themselves nicely to the divisions of the child's investigations. Three sides of a cardboard box will do the job well. Suggest that everything be blocked in first with pencil. Then, when the display is in its final form, a felt pen can be used. The top of the left section is a good place to write in the hypotheses or scientific questions the investigation sought to answer. The lower half might carry a description of the methods used in carrying out the project. The right-hand panel can show the investigator's name, grade, and any other required information. (Perhaps this is an appropriate time for you to consult the school bulletin you posted on the refrigerator.) On the same panel, your child might put his or her conclusions—but only those based on the data. Opinions just do not count, no matter how sure the investigator may be. The body of the data or a model can be put on the center panel of the display. Try not to get possessive about the project at this point. (Or at any other, for that matter.) Let it end up looking like exactly what it is: the beginning work of a youngster investigating the use of inductive reasoning and the scientific method.

Finally

Both of you will probably feel considerable satisfaction when the project is completed. But, if the project is to be entered in competition, your child may also be wondering how successful it's going to be. This depends, of course, on the criteria on which it's to be judged. Some fairs publish their criteria, and, in this case, you'll probably find them on the refrigerator with your other science fair information. Otherwise, try checking the project against the general criteria we offer. (See Box.) They will give

How Does the Project Measure Up?

Scientific Thought
- Does the project follow the scientific method? (hypothesis, method, data, conclusion)
- Does the project illustrate controlled experimentation?
- Does it represent real study and effort?
- Does it make appropriate comparisons?
- Does it form conclusions based only on the data gathered?
- Does the project show that the child is familiar with the topic?

Originality
- Does the project demonstrate some ideas arrived at by the child?
- Does the project show a high degree of accomplishment? Is the degree of accomplishment consistent with the student's age level?
- Is the project primarily the work of the child? Does it give that impression?

Thoroughness
- Does the project tell a complete story?
- Are all the parts of the project well done, including the visual display and the oral presentation?

Technical Skill
- Is the project physically sound and durably constructed? Will it stand normal wear and tear?
- Does the project show effort and craftsmanship by the student?

Clarity
- Are the labels clear, correct, and easy to read?
- Is the objective likely to be understood by one not technically trained in the subject area?
- Does the project attract attention?
- Is attention sustained by the project?
- Is attention focused on the objective?

you and your child an idea of what modifications, if any, ought to be made in the project.

As part of the judging process, your child may be asked to explain the project to the judges or to present it to the class. Those in charge usually try hard to make the presenter feel comfortable in this situation, but a dress rehearsal might be a wise move. Simply encourage your child to go through the project as if explaining it to someone totally unfamiliar with its purpose and development. Start with his or her name.

Then give the title of the project and explain how interest in it was first aroused. The child might then simply talk his or her way through the project, step by step. The more comfortable your child is, the easier it will be not simply to read from the project write-up.

Undertaking a project for a school show or competition can be a daunting prospect for young children, especially if they are expected to work without the teacher's constant guidance. A little preparation, however, can assist a par-

ent in reassuming the role of guide. We hear much today about the value of individualizing education, and it's important to recognize the part a parent can play in this process. There simply is no match for the parent-as-teacher in working with youngsters, and there can be no more fitting place for learning to occur and no more loving individualization to be found than at the hands of a concerned parent. Not only does learning occur, but the opportunity for sharing is enhanced, as parent and child set out on the road of inquiry together.

Did Billy Gene Do This Project Himself?

Stephen A. Henderson, director of the Model Laboratory School, Eastern Kentucky University, Richmond, recently wrote S&C with comments on a big science fair question.—ED.

Having supervised hundreds of projects, directed many fairs, and judged scored of others, I'm very familiar with the question, "How much of this work did the student do?" It's not hard to see why teachers ask it, but the importance given this question may cause us to ignore one of the greatest benefits a science project can offer—the opportunity for child and parent (or other adult) to work together to produce a project in which both can take pride. This message was made even clearer to me when one of our elementary teachers received the following letter:

This is to certify that Billy Gene performed all workmanship on his Solar

Water Heater project himself, with advice but no other assistance except that noted. The measuring, sawing, drilling, painting, soldering, screwing, and hammering are all his handiwork. Throughout the project he has been required to explain the basic principles involved. While he articulates them poorly, I am positive his understanding is thorough. (We didn't discuss finer points such as refraction, wave lengths.)

If his project merits an award it might encourage him in further study. However, my greater motivation in the several projects we have worked on is not blue ribbons but promotion of his already keen thirst for knowledge. Close scrutiny will reveal many imperfections, but the project is still darn good for an eleven-year-old. Without this letter I feared you might think the project done for him, instead of by him. A lesser project would not have challenged him.

Granddad bent the tubing (he tried first), drove one stubborn nail, cut the

plexiglass, and soldered one tube to the bucket (to demonstrate technique). Billy Gene did the rest.

I confess to too much advice in helping him condense his volumes of poster material. He had accumulated enough pages of drawings, tool and material lists, data, principles, and conclusions to nearly paper a wall of your classroom instead of make one poster. If time were not running out, I would have advised less.
Sincerely,
Eugene Spurlock (Granddad)

The letter reinforces my feelings about adults' helping with science projects. This eleven year old probably learned more science as he worked with his grandfather than anyone could have taught him in the classroom. Perhaps more important, the experience deepened a family relationship that will last a lifetime. Hurrah for science projects, willing kids, and granddads!

As this school year progresses, are you going to join the teacher chorus of "I wish I could get parents more involved in science?" Or are you going to take the initiative and get them involved?

Parental involvement is one of the hallmarks of every exemplary science program. Parents can make the difference between a great program and a poor one by supplying resources, donating time, and enhancing motivation. But first you need to let them know they're needed.

Begin early in the school year by introducing yourself. Write a personal letter which describes your background, attitudes, and goals for the science program. Mail it to each household, or hand it to parents at the first school open house.

The Invitation

A questionnaire asking for support in specific areas can accompany this letter, or follow it later in the semester. Emphasize the importance of the parents' role in creating the best possible program for their children, and give them lots of options to choose from. It's smart to set up your list in a way that implies you expect each parent to do *something*— then their only decision is choosing which role to take.

The options on your list can include helping in the classroom, whether on a one-time or a regular basis; visiting the classroom as a guest speaker, or inviting someone else to visit; donating money for science equipment; subscribing to science periodicals for the classroom; helping organize the science fair, or serving on a science fair committee; and donating household chemicals and lab supplies. Leave an open category ("Other") for contributions you may not have thought of. But be sure to keep the format simple and concise, so parents will read it, fill it out, and send it back.

SCIENCE FAIRS: A Family Affair

The Meeting

Follow these initial contacts by meeting with parents as a group. This meeting can be part of a scheduled open house, or you can call a special meeting to discuss plans for the science fair. In either case, plan to sit down once with all the parents early in the year—perhaps in October or November.

During the meeting, be sure to cover the following points:
- Guidelines for selecting projects
- Guidelines for constructing projects
- Guidelines for parental guidance and involvement
- Criteria for judging
- The need for PTA support

Use this time to repeat your request for specific assistance, and try to get each parent committed to some task before they leave the meeting. Invite and encourage questions from parents and other guests.

Have sample science projects on hand. The winners from last year's fair are a good choice. If your meeting involves parents of different grade levels, have projects from each level for them to see. Parents will enjoy examining the projects before and after the formal portion of the meeting.

PTA Involvement

With science becoming a national priority, it is reasonable to expect PTA support for your science program. But don't leave it to chance: here too, communication is the key.

Meet with the president of the organization early in the year and explain your needs. Be prepared with specifics about the cost and use of each item, and prioritize your list. Then follow up on your requests.

The benefits of parental involvement will not be limited to the science department. Parents will gain satisfaction and experience, and other departments in the school will also pick up volunteers, because of the enthusiasm you've generated.

Maybe this year, your school's science fair will make everyone feel like a member of a winning team!

AVA PUGH
And
CHARLES PRYOR
Northeast Louisiana University
Monroe, Louisiana

WHOEVER Invented the Science Fair . . .

Linda H. Sittig

Whoever invented the science fair was certainly not the parent of a first grader. I speak with the voice of experience, having recently survived our family's first encounter with a science fair.

When our six-year-old daughters announced that they wanted to enter a project in their school's science fair, I inwardly cringed. Remembering how difficult math and science had always been for me, I had a feeling that this project could turn out to be a colossal headache. The enthusiasm on their faces, however, made me ignore the little voice inside me begging to say *no*, and I asked them what project they had in mind.

I would probably have favored some of the experiments with magnets I remembered from my elementary science days or perhaps a project on different types of clouds. But the girls said they wanted to build their own bird feeders and paint them different colors to see if birds liked one color more than another, and I asked myself how complicated that could possibly be. We would construct two bird feeders, spray paint them, add birdseed, and then watch to see where the birds would eat.

Enter now Dad upon the scene. Since my husband is a junior high science teacher, he had his own ideas about how a science fair project should be carried out. Sitting down as a family, we began to discuss the battle plan, and I heard him uttering phrases like "data retrieval charts" and "correct observational procedure." Worse, he went on to say that our daughters would need to weigh and record the precise amount of seeds, in grams, that the birds consumed each day. I raised some objections based on the academic capabilities of six year olds. But I finally had to capitulate and agree that if you decide to enter a science fair, you do the project right, or not at all—even if you are only six years old.

Needless to say, all free time during the next two weeks was consumed by the project, and I for one felt enormous relief when the finished product was deposited on a table at the science fair. But looking back now, I realize that my children benefited from this experience in a number of tangible ways. They practiced math skills by weighing the birdseed daily on a balance scale (and exercised their fine motor coordination as they adjusted the weights of the balance). Large muscle control came into play as the girls banged away with hammers, and language skills increased as they read books on how to build bird feeders and how to feed birds. They even practiced their handwriting because they kept a daily log (AKA data retrieval chart) of their activities. Most important, they had the experience of getting an idea and following it through to its conclusion.

I learned a valuable lesson too: children are often capable of achieving more than we give them credit for. Although our daughters could not have handled their science experiment without adult supervision, the credit for conceiving and carrying out the project belonged to them. And this realization suggested a response to the dilemma that troubles many parents and teachers. How can we challenge children without applying too much academic pressure?

The key to the success of the science fair project seemed to lie in the fact that our daughters took the initiative—it was not forced upon them—and they were given the freedom to pursue their own idea. Of course, children do not always come up with ideas of their own that they are eager to pursue. But if adults could be more sensitive to what interests children or students, we could guide—not push—them into activities that they would find challenging and exciting. And if we could be more sensitive, we would nurture, not discourage, the inquisitiveness without which children will never reach their full potential.

Science fairs do come only once a year (I'm still thankful for small mercies), but there are many other opportunities for us to encourage our children's minds to grow. We have only to take advantage of them.

By the way, red seems to be a very popular color with birds.

Linda H. Sittig is a reading specialist with the Fairfax County (Virginia) Public Schools.

Science fairs are exciting. Teachers and students generally agree that they are worth every bit of the hard work that goes into them. But what about those students who choose not to do an independent science project? Chances are a student who is turned on to science by one of the nontraditional events described in this section will turn up later in the olympiads and other competitive programs. But the main advantage of these programs is they offer every student a chance to be a scientist, if only for a day.

Beyond the Science Fair

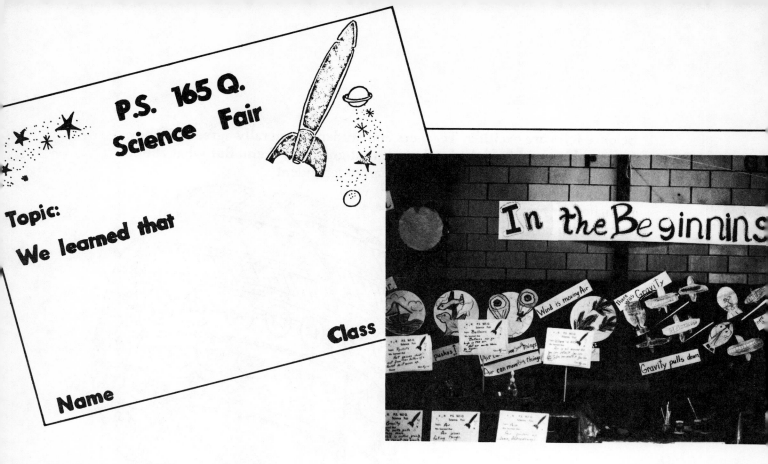

(Above left) A concept card, which children used to describe what they had learned in doing their Teach-In projects. (Above right) Some of the projects students completed for the 1984 Teach-In.

Earth in Space: A Science Teach-In

By Kristine Marames

Is a science fair your school's outstanding science event of the year? At P. S. 165 in Flushing, New York, we think we've discovered something better. Our annual Teach-In has all the excitement of a science fair—without the edge of competitiveness—and it turns everyone who attends into a participant. Here's how it works.

Each year at P. S. 165, we emphasize a different area of science (some recent areas have included the environment, water, and change), and each student studies a related topic and makes a project. At the end of the year, we organize the Teach-In, a school-wide event lasting a day and a half, during which students share, with schoolmates and parents, what they've learned in doing their projects. In 1984 the subject area was space.

We began with a committee consisting of the principal and several other teachers, which selected space as that year's focus. Since I was the science teacher, I was responsible for breaking the topic down into six subtopics, one for each grade.

Using the New York City curriculum bulletins as guides, I chose topics that would not overlap for each grade. Earth in space was selected as the large topic and divided into six areas.

To give the various topics a second unifying theme, students at each grade level were to study how the U.S. space program applied to their subtopic; for example, the fourth grade studied the missions to the Moon.

In December, we held meetings to discuss and select activities for each grade. (See box opposite for a list of subjects and projects.) We decided that every grade would use a computer for one exhibit, write computer programs, and create games for other students to see and play.

During this period, I kept in contact with the other teachers, providing them with the materials and information they needed.

While students worked on their projects, the faculty planned assembly programs. We ordered films from NASA and elsewhere and showed them from November through February. Being able to watch a space shuttle lift-off and landing on television added to the children's excitement. Many children wrote to the astronauts after seeing the flight, telling them about the Teach-In and asking specific questions about the space flight.

As the day of the fair approached, each class chose demonstrators to tell about the projects. And as each project was completed, the children prepared a large concept card for it, containing a relevant drawing, the problem posed by the project, and a summary of what they had learned.

Preparation for the actual display of class projects took two days. Teachers organized the gym into sections, one for each grade, with easels and movable chalkboards. We designed the floor plan,

See TEACH-IN page 57

Suggested Activities and Topics for Space Science Teach-In

Kindergarten: In the Beginning
Air
- How pinwheels work
- How air can slow things down
- How air pushes things

Balloons
- The first human being's journey into the air
- Making models with balloons and milk cartons

Astronauts
- What space flight was like for the early astronauts

Making a large mural on flight

Grade 1: What Is in the Sky?
Rockets
- Making a poster on rockets
- Writing stories about being in a rocket

Kites
- Studying kinds of kites

The Sun
- The types and functions of visors
- Writing and acting in a skit about the sun (presented by shadow puppets)

Clouds
- The different types of clouds
- Making models of clouds with cotton balls

Planets
- Making a poster of the planets
- Making a cardboard model of a rocket (which would actually be a travel agency that provides information about trips to the planets)
- Revolution and rotation demonstration

Constellation peep show
- Making models of constellations with oatmeal boxes, in which holes have been punched to represent stars

Moon
- Keeping experience charts
- Drawing pictures of the phases of the Moon

Space dictionary
- Making and playing space-related puzzles

Grade 2: Traveling in Air
Constructing paper airplanes
Parachutes
- Learning about the different types
- Learning about how parachutes operate

Grade 3: The Earth and Sun
Weather station
- Learning about different weather instruments
    Anemometer
    Thermometer
    Barometer
- Learning how to use weather instruments
- Learning about weather forecasting

Learning about different ways to tell time
- Sundials
- Other instruments

Learning about becoming an astronaut (based on NASA's Elementary Activities)
- Testing peripheral vision
- Testing reaction time

Learning about different kinds of spacecraft
- Aspects of the craft that protect the astronaut
- Various models of spacecraft

Grade 4: The Moon
Learning about the models of uncrewed spacecraft
- Lunar module
- Saturn rocket

Writing and acting in a skit about the landing of Apollo 11
Learning about the lunar surface
- Making clay models of the Moon
- Making a model that demonstrates craters forming

Designing models of future lunar colonies

Grade 5: The Solar System
Making models of the solar system
Learning about possible colonies on other planets
- Studying the characteristics of the various planets
- Requirements for colonies

Learning about the Kennedy Space Center
- Making a model of the Center
- Describing the Space Center

Reading (or writing) biographies of people who have contributed to our knowledge of space

Grade 6: The Universe
Building and demonstrating a telescope
Making models of stars that show their colors and sizes
Making a chart that shows the layers of the atmosphere
Demonstrating Newton's Laws of Motion
The Sun and ancient humans
- Learning about how human beings once worshiped the Sun
- Learning about superstitions related to the Sun
- Studying the zodiac

Katy Kelly

Consumer Fair: A Cure........

for the Science Fair Blues

Spring should be a time of rejuvenated optimism, renewed vigor, and hearty self-congratulation upon successfully surviving another winter. However, in classrooms across the nation, science teachers are faced with the seasonal malady known as Science Fair Syndrome (SFS). The victims of SFS often complain of low student motivational levels, high incidences of uncontrolled variables, and hallucinatory visions of papier-mache volcanoes. If you share these symptoms, why not try a consumer fair as an alternative to a traditional science fair?

The basic premise of the consumer fair is that we are all purchasers of goods and services. From the toddler begging for a penny for the gumball machine to an adult making a decision on the purchase of a cemetery plot, the acquisition and spending of money is a basic fact of life. Our economy encourages consumption by young people, but often these young consumers do not have the skills and knowledge necessary to buy wisely. Consumer fair projects encourage students to use scientific investigation skills learned in the classroom as a means to becoming more independent and intelligent consumers.

In the consumer fair scheme, the students are led through a series of steps to arrive at their own choice of project topic and investigation. The first step is a visit to the neighborhood grocery store with its variety of grocery and other consumer products. The students list ten foods and ten non-food products and three brands of each product on a form which I provide. They then narrow down their list of products until they have chosen the one product of greatest interest to them. This single product represented by three different brands for the purposes of comparison becomes the subject of their project. Next students decide which of the many aspects of their product they wish to investigate. The aspects might include: weight, volume, number of items, packaging, effectiveness, or taste. Their final step in this preliminary stage is to formulate a question (hypothesis) about the aspect they will use to compare the three product brands. An example of an investigative question is: Which brand of diaper, brand X, Y, or Z, actually absorbs the most moisture?

Students use the scientific method to search for answers. Consumer projects offer the opportunity for them to construct a hypothesis from a question, identify and control variables, design and conduct an experiment, and collect and analyze data (see Figure 1). Students often need assistance as they develop their experimental design. During this phase, the teacher serves as resource

Figure 1:
Investigation Set-Up Sheet

Product Investigated:_____

_____

Three Brands Compared: _____

_____

Question about Product to be

Answered:_____

_____

1. **Hypothesis:**

2. **Manipulated Variable:**

3. **Responding Variable:**

4. **Controlled Variable:**

5. **Equipment:**

6. **Procedure:**

7. **Data Collected:**

8. **Hypothesis Check:**

9. **Conclusion:**

person and facilitator, answering questions and offering advice. The actual experiments may be conducted in or out of class. While some experiments require equipment and the use of process and measuring skills, others such as blind tests for taste preference, emphasize the use of subjects and proper sampling and control techniques.

In addition to the data gathered during their experiments, the students also compare the tested brands by doing a cost analysis (Figure 2). They compare the three brands using one quantitative aspect, such as volume, weight, or number of items, divided into each brand's cost. The resulting per unit cost is used to determine which brand is the best buy.

The students bring experimental data they collect in the form of graphs, charts, conclusions, and experimental procedures on posters. The posters, the three brands of the product used for comparison, and the materials used to conduct the experiment are combined as a display. These displays make up the consumer fair. Teachers evaluate the projects according to the scoring criteria in Figure 3.

Consumer fairs are educational, interesting, motivating, and fun. The activities provide reinforcement of skills taught in the science classroom and help students become knowledgeable and independent consumers. Most important, consumer fairs illustrate that science and the methods of science are relevant to students' everyday lives.

DONALD J. NELSON
Ridgewood School
Rock Island, Illinois

References

Burzler, D. R. "Be a Super Shopper." *Arithmetic Teacher* 25:40-4; March 1978.

Carlock, L. L. "Will Your Students Be Effective Consumers?" *Business Education Forum* 38:58-61; April/May 1984.

Foxworth, E. H. "How to Spend That Hard-Earned Dime." *Teacher* 94:93-6; January 1977.

Kleefield, James. "Teaching Consumer Skills." *Learning* 9:32-3; September 1980.

Opsata, Margaret. "Consumer Awareness." *Instructor* 89:154-6; February 1980.

Padilla, Michael. "Using Consumer Science to Develop Experimental Techniques." *Science and Children* 18:22-3; January 1981.

Seese, John W. "Don't Throw In the Towel—Test It!" *The Science Teacher* 51:28-9; April 1984.

Figure 2: Cost Analysis

When comparing several brands of the same product, a consumer is often interested in which is the "best buy." You can figure any relative costs of several brands of the same product by doing a *cost analysis*.

Directions: You first decide on one aspect of the product that you will use to compare all the brands. You should use *volume, weight,* or *number of items* for this comparison. Then fill in the chart below using the brands you are comparing.

Brands	Cost	Volume, Weight, or Number of Items
1.		
2.		
3.		

You will need to do some dividing. Divide the cost of the brand into its volume, weight, or number of items to find the *per unit cost* for each of your brands. The *per unit cost* tells you how much product you get for one cent. Use the formula below to help.

$$\text{Cost} \sqrt{\overline{\text{Volume, Weight, or No. of Items}}}^{\,\text{Per Unit Cost}}$$

Repeat the procedure for all the brands being compared. Then fill in the chart below to identify which brand is the best buy.

Brand	Per Unit Cost	Best Buy
1.		
2.		
3.		

Figure 3: Project Scoresheet

_____ 1-5	**A) Project Set-Up** • Question investigated well thought out • Investigation procedure well designed • Investigation followed as designed
_____ 1-5	**B) Project Results** • Quality data collected • Hypothesis check supported by data • Data displayed using charts or graphs • Conclusions made from data clearly stated
_____ 1-5	**C) Project Appearance** • Posters complete and neatly printed • Display well organized • Display informative and understandable • Product brands displayed
_____ 1-5	**D) Brand-Cost Analysis** • Brands correctly compared • Correct calculations • Best buy data clearly charted or graphed
_____ 1-5	**E) Project Effort** • Project complete and on time
_____ = 5-25	**Total Score** **1st Place** = 23–25 points, **2nd place** = 20–22 points **3rd Place** = 17–19 points, **4th place** = 14–16 points

"**M**om, I don't like science —I love it!" This was the exclamation of a five-year-old girl who recently participated in the activities that made up We Love Science Day at Clarion University of Pennsylvania. And she was not alone. Numerous elementary school students and their parents and other relatives shared her enthusiasm not only last summer (and the one before) during the celebration of We Love Science Day, which was the culmination of a

We Love Science Day

By Lynne Kepler

workshop for primary school teachers, but also during home and school classroom projects happening in the fall and winter. Thus, in numerous Pennsylvania classrooms and homes, We Love Science *Day* turned into We Love Science *Year.*

The participants for the day-long celebration—about 30 elementary school children and about 15 parents and grandparents—were recruited through newspaper ads. One day late during each of the last two summers, the children and their escorting relatives joined a group of primary school teachers at Clarion University in a morning and afternoon of activities demonstrating electricity, plant and animal life, the senses, health, sound, weather, and simple machines. The concepts and skills taught by many hands-on science activities were reinforced with songs, stories, and puppet shows.

Science, Science, Everywhere

Both summers, We Love Science Day was the work of the teachers from all over Pennsylvania who were involved in a course, Creative Integration of Science in Elementary Education

(CISEE), offered as part of a statewide teacher inservice program by the Pennsylvania Science Teacher Education Program. Among other precepts, the course teaches that, because basic science skills such as observing, inferring, classifying, measuring, communicating, and interpreting data cut across curricular lines, children can practice them throughout the school day in unified and purposeful learning situations. In addition, CISEE emphasizes parental involvement and suggests ways in which teachers can help mothers and fathers find concrete ways to do science with their children outside of the classroom.

Funded by the state's Higher Education Assistance Agency, the CISEE workshops got started in 1985 when they ran three weeks, serving 26 teachers. The program originally served only the early elementary teachers; in 1986, in response to requests, it was restructured to meet the needs of teachers across the elementary school curriculum from kindergarten to sixth grade. This summer's group of instructors was about the same size as that participating in 1985, but it met only two weeks at Clarion; participants spent the third

week back at their individual schools. There the teachers put into practice what they had learned and shared their new knowledge and approaches with other teachers.

At their own schools, the CISEE teachers conducted two half-day We

Love Science Day sessions, one in the morning and one in the afternoon. Groups of about six parents and children, accompanied by a teacher, rotated through four activity-oriented science stations in the morning session and four more stations in the afternoon. At each of the eight stations, the children participated in a hands-on science activity. At the same time, parents joined in related activities that they could later enjoy with their children at home.

At the plant science station, for example, children began a plant growth investigation. They prepared "pine cone trees" by rolling pine cones in potting soil and grass seed. As the children were making predictions about their trees' growth and listening to a story about trees, their parents learned how to make simple terrariums at home using liter-sized soft drink bottles as containers.

While the students were learning how inclined planes reduce effort, parents were learning how to help their children recognize other inclined planes. And as the young worked with toy trucks, sand buckets, pulleys, and inclined planes, the parent group went on a simple machines scavenger hunt, learning to recognize many everyday items as belonging to that category—ramps, sliding boards, scissors, even elbows! At another station, children played Simon Says to discover how their vision helps them maintain their balance: they toppled off one foot much faster with eyes closed than with them open. Parents performed similar balancing acts to stimulate future discussions at home on balance, lighting, and safety.

Besides learning about some science projects that would work well at home, parents received a calendar listing other extracurricular science activities. Many parents are eager to do such activities with their children but puzzled as to how to get started or exactly what to do. Parents who play scientific games with their children are serving a vital role in helping to reinforce the skills children learn in school, the same skills they will need for learning throughout their lifetimes. (See McIntyre, 1980, for further specifics.)

Three Cheers for Science!

We Love Science Day was popular with all participants—children, parents, and teachers. Hands-on activities pique children's interest in science (an essential first step) and enhance overall learning of basic skills; they should obviously be part of the regular science curriculum, but they are even more powerful if they are also part of life outside school. (See Mechling and Oliver, 1983.)

Start your own We Love Science Day to stimulate hands-on science both at home and at school. Many CISEE teachers have found their colleagues as well as parent-teacher associations willing allies in sponsoring and coordinating such celebrations. And don't be afraid to start small—maybe half a day, maybe just sending home an integrated science calendar with activities that build on your lesson plans.

By next year, you'll be on your way to establishing a We Love Science Day tradition in your school.

References
McIntyre, Margaret. (1980, January). Early childhood: Involving parents in science. *S&C*, 17(4), 46–47.
Mechling, Kenneth R., and Oliver, Donna. (1983). *Science teaches basic skills: Handbook I*. Washington: NSTA.
_____. (1983). *What research says about elementary school science*. Washington: NSTA.

Lynne Kepler is assistant director of the Teacher Education Center at Clarion University of Pennsylvania, Clarion. Photograph courtesy of the author.

TEACH-IN *Continued from page 52*

Continued from page 52

and the students made charts to help create a festive atmosphere.

The auditorium was booked for films and speakers during the Teach-In. Some classes began their visits by going to the gym to view exhibits and speak with demonstrators, while other classes started with the auditorium. The children had sent invitations to parents so that they too could attend the event.

At the 1984 Teach-In, as at all of these yearly events, the children's demonstrations were an outgrowth of their work in science for the year. Students became teachers, demonstrating to their parents and peers what they had learned and what they had experienced firsthand. Focusing on one area of science—rather than covering many different topics with individual projects—created enthusiasm and unity within the school. After this Teach-In, too, many students asked the standard question, "What are we doing next year?"

Resources
For information on obtaining the elementary science curriculum guides, contact the New York City Board of Education, Publication Sales Office, 131 Livingston St., Rm 613, Brooklyn, NY 11201; tel. 718-596-4902.

And for additional suggestions for space fair projects, refer to the following:
Caballero, Jane. (1979). *Aerospace projects for young children*. Atlanta: Humanics Limited.
Housel, David, and Housel, Doreen. (19xx). *Exploring science K-6 through aviation/aerospace concepts*. Lansing, Mich.: Aerospace Education Council of Michigan.
NASA. (1977). *Elementary school aerospace activities—A resource for teachers*. Washington: NASA.

Kristine Marames is now teaching fifth grade students in the Alpha Program for the Gifted at Public School 165 in Flushing, New York. Illustrations on page 36 courtesy of the author.

—Thomas M. Staley, courtesy of Montgomery County, Md.

Meet Me at the Fair

by William G. Lamb and Peter Brown

*Science fairs should
be more like
county fairs.*

During the mid to late 1960s, support for science fairs waned to the point where many sponsors just plain got out of the science fair business. Every teacher knows what science fairs are: research project competitions in which students present their results on three-sided exhibit boards a maximum of 75 cm deep, 120 cm wide, and 270 cm tall. Right? These science fairs follow the rules and regulations specified by the International Science and Engineering Fair (ISEF) as administered by Science Service in Washington, D.C.

Among other definitions for "fair," my old battered dictionary gives the closest one for both science fairs and county fairs: "a competitive exhibition (as of farm products)." I must admit that I was surprised by the emphasis in the definition because my idea of a county fair is as much rides and entertainment as pigs and pickles winning blue ribbons. In addition to these contests, county fairs have something else that traditional science fairs often lack: joy, sparkle, and diversity.

Last year in Oregon, a consortium of groups got together to start a state science fair after many years without one. We wanted to have a real fair in the county fair sense with events and activities in addition to the typical ISEF research competition. But first, our event needed a name. We couldn't use *science fair* because too many people, we thought, associated those words with unpleasant competition. So, after much discussion, we called the 3-day event the Northwest Science Exposition.

Brainstorming produced plans for a series of events. First, we would have a research competition, affiliated with the ISEF and run according to its rules and format. We called it a research competition to stress that it was only one part of the overall exposition.

We also arranged a noncompetitive display of student projects at the Oregon Museum of Science and Industry (OMSI). Many students, especially younger students, we decided, would rather exhibit their work and receive recognition for it in a noncompetitive, unjudged forum. Students could display research, but we also encouraged other kinds of projects—familiar models and demonstrations of well-known scientific principles as well as more creative science-art projects and diaries of nature trails. Originally, we thought this event would attract mostly middle schoolers, but we soon found that a significant number of high schoolers, including many who had done bona fide "competitive" research projects, opted to exhibit their work at the noncompetitive show.

In our third event, an "olympics," teams of students challenged one another in the high school science big three: biology, chemistry, and physics. Each of the olympics began with a quiz in which every team took a written test. Team members cooperated in answering the items. Then the top four teams competed in a college-bowl-type verbal quiz. Except for the quiz bowl, each olympic event was unique. I describe some of them in the box accompanying this article.

We also arranged a series of tours

—*Kathy Middleton*

—Kathy Middleton

to sites of scientific interest, including the Washington Park Zoo (students got to go "backstage" as well as view the animals out front), the Oregon Graduate Center (various research labs), the Regional Primate Research Center (research labs and a Macaque colony), CH2MHill Civil Engineering firm, and the National Weather Service.

Finally, students could sign up for workshops at OMSI in forensic science, microbial genetics, computer flight simulation, and computer graphics and music. One day at the exposition, Astronomy Day, featured an OMSI planetarium educator offering workshops and shows. Some students opted to see videotapes from the *Voyager* missions.

In addition, the Lane County (Oregon) Educational Service District provided a portable planetarium, and students and teachers could attend science films during the day at OMSI. To avoid the problem of students having nothing to do on Friday night and to promote social interaction among students from the different schools, we scheduled a barbecue, a physics demonstration, and a dance, complete with a very live band.

Putting on this extravaganza posed a number of problems and required the close cooperation of many groups of people. Fortunately, the Expo was sponsored by a consortium including the Oregon Science Teachers Association (OSTA), the Portland section of the American Chemical Society (ACS), the Oregon section of the American Association of Physics Teachers (AAPT), the Northwest Association of Marine Educators (NAME), the

At the starting line

Step right up and try your luck at the fair with these team competitions. Your students may not come up with a kewpie doll for their efforts, but they will have every bit as much fun at these science fair activities as they would at the county fair. And they may learn a bit of science, too.

- *Biology charades.* Each four-student team uses one demonstrator and three interpreters to demonstrate as many randomly drawn biological terms as possible in 30 min.
- *Acid titration.* Each team determines the equivalent weight of an unknown solid acid using a buret and a standardized base solution the team brings to the Expo.
- *Ethanol purification.* Given a 125-mL aqueous solution of ethanol, each team prepares a 50-mL sample of ethanol. Award prizes based on proof. In our competition a group of eighth graders enrolled in IPS beat a group of high school students.
- *Maximum density of an aqueous solution.* Each team brings its own solid. Have the teams exchange solids and then make solutions with deionized water you provide. After 20 min., teams filter their solutions and determine density with a hydrometer.
- *Qualitative analysis.* Give each team seven numbered test tubes, each containing an unknown cation. Teams must identify the ions.
- *Paper airplane time of flight.* Each team designs paper airplanes according to rules available before the olympics. Add times of flight for each team's planes; the highest team total wins.
- *Laser shoot.* Place a HeNe laser 1 m from a semicircular dish of water. Place a target on the other side of the dish and 6 m from the laser. Each team must figure the angle of refraction and predict the position of the laser beam on the target for a given angle of the semicircular dish. —W. L./P. B.

William G. Lamb teaches chemistry and physics at Oregon Episcopal School, 6300 S.W. Nicol Rd., Portland, OR 97223. Peter Brown is a teaching associate at the Oregon Museum of Science and Industry, 4015 S.W. Canyon Rd., Portland, OR 97221.

Oregon State Department of Education, and the Oregon Museum of Science and Industry. This cross-fertilization has been important because, although many of the same teachers belong to OSTA and NAME, there is very little overlap among OSTA, ACS, and AAPT. Although the Expo would probably have been easier to stage with fewer interests represented and a well-financed dictator delegating the tasks, the give-and-take of planning meetings and our mutual delight in finally executing the Expo helped all of us build vital professional networks.

Coordinating so many activities at three sites separated by several kilometers proved to be pretty challenging, but came off with only a few hitches. We arranged for shuttle bus service between the sites. Except for students who tried to take part in both the research competition (which ran a little ahead of schedule) and the olympics (which ran a little behind schedule), most students got where they wanted to go on time.

In its first year, the Expo served 33 schools and more than 500 students. Most schools participated in a variety of the activities. More than 60 percent of the teachers returned a questionnaire evaluating the Expo. The general consensus? The Expo was just dandy and would have been dandier with better organization.

We're quite proud of our first annual Expo, which was supported by generous grants from the Swindells Fund of the Oregon Community Foundation and the Winningstad Chair Fund of the Oregon Episcopal School. We look forward to the next, which will be held in Hillsboro (Oregon) High School, April 12–13, 1985. We are especially happy that all the major events will be at one site. It's the combination of individual research and team competition, noncompetitive exhibits, films, tours, workshops, and social events that makes the Northwest Science Exposition a real science fair. ∎

Pointing the Way for Young Researchers

by Lynn W. Glass

Sometimes students have a hard time sifting through the rules of a science fair to come up with a project that pleases both the judges and themselves. Here in Iowa, a strong support organization guides students through their early days in research. From before project planning to the national meeting of the American Junior Academy of Science, the Iowa Junior Academy of Science backs its young researchers.

Each fall the Iowa Junior Academy conducts a "how to" workshop for high school students and teachers who are interested in getting a science research project started. The workshop helps students define a manageable research topic, locate resources (both people and print), and learn how to present findings. Other teachers and successful student researchers run the workshops.

We then introduce the young scientists to a skill that will come in quite handy if they go on in research: writing research grant proposals. We encourage all Iowa secondary school students to complete a two-page grant application form, and we award research support of up to $200 for a project.

Science students in Iowa seem to be always busy—at science fairs, science symposia, science olympics, university research participation projects, and various other science competitions. The Iowa Junior Academy of Science publicizes these events and recognizes the winners. At its annual meeting, the Iowa Academy of Science highlights award-winning students from the many state science events of the

Lynn W. Glass directs the Iowa Junior Academy of Science and is a professor of secondary education, N156 Quadrangle, Iowa State University, Ames, IA 50011.

preceding year. In addition, the director of each event nominates a select few students to compete for our Junior Academy's highest honor—two expense-paid trips to the annual meetings of the American Association for the Advancement of Science and the American Junior Academy of Science. The students vie for the awards by presenting a poster paper and oral research report. The governor of Iowa usually comes to honor all these deserving students.

The 1983–1984 school year marked the first annual Outstanding Science Student Award program sponsored by the Iowa Junior Academy of Science and the Iowa Academy of Science. Nearly 400 senior students from 500 Iowa high schools received a bronze medallion for their excellence in science.

We're also excited about our first amusement park physics project this fall. More than 2000 junior high students are learning about physics while having fun on 12 different amusement park rides. Plans are currently underway to expand this popular event to include even more students next fall.

Funding for our many events and activities comes from three sources. Private enterprise covers a large portion of our expenses. A competitive grant from the American Association for the Advancement of Science pays about half of our student research grant program. Dues and other sources of income to the Iowa Academy of Science are the third source of support for the Junior Academy.

We like to think of the Iowa Junior Academy of Science as a training ground for a new generation of scientists. Don't be surprised if a disproportionate number of the next crop of Nobel laureates in science hail from the Hawkeye State. ∎

SCIENCE CHALLENGE

Olympic Achievement for Your Science Program

By Donald E. Maxwell and Glenn Berkheimer

Do you want to motivate teachers to teach and students to learn more science? Do you want your students to view science positively and have a continued interest in scientific and technological issues? Do you want students to recognize and develop their scientific talents? Sounds impossible? Not if you organize a school- or district-wide challenge.

Scientific Olympics

We modeled the science challenge after the Olympics. But where the Olympics focus on individual and team *athletic* prowess in a competitive setting, our science challenge focuses on students' abilities to collect, organize, and analyze data; try their hand at problem solving; and show an understanding of science concepts and principles in a competitive setting.

By carefully designing the science challenge, you can expect some of these important benefits.

- The quantity and quality of the science teaching at your school will increase.
- All students will have a positive experience with science beyond the classroom. This involvement will encourage them to continue taking science courses.
- The science challenge will serve as a more accurate measure of students' process skills than traditional testing programs. Elementary school students with previous hands-on experience will be more successful in the science challenge than those without the previous experience.
- The competition will encourage good

public relations. It exposes the community to the elementary school science program; it introduces the parents to the objectives of the program, to the teachers, and to the principals.

A Variety of Events

The philosophy of the science challenge is that designing a variety of events for the competition will stimulate and challenge all science students. Offering students a variety of events encourages both the typically successful and the typically less-successful science students to compete and to win—thus decreasing the negative aspects of competition. (Primary grade events could be included without competition and instead could demonstrate childrens' mastery of skills and concepts just by "doing.")

Getting Organized

Once you have decided that a science challenge is a worthwhile venture, your next step is to establish your objectives. Then identify the science activities that have promise as challenge events. For example, a fifth grade "Energy Sources" unit of the Science Curriculum Improvement Study (SCIS) program could be made into an event in which students demonstrate their knowledge of energy transfer. (See the "Spheres to Sliders" chapter developed into an event about mass movement.)

Once you have determined the potential events, you must decide on the following components of each event:

- necessary materials
- rules
- directions for coordinators and judges
- scoring materials
- advanced information needed by teachers, students and parents.

Possible Challenge Events

You might make the Elementary Science Study (ESS) unit "Mystery Powders" a challenge event entitled "Identifying Chemical Unknowns" that uses the same materials as those for the "Mystery Powders" unit. You would prepare three mystery systems, each containing two or more of the EES mystery powders. Then, you would place three mystery systems at a series of independent stations so that a number of students could do the activity at the same time. The rules for this event might be to use only the materials provided at each station to identify each of the components in each of the three mystery systems.

Students would have 20 minutes to complete the activity and 10 minutes to organize their data and write up a report indicating their findings and the evidence for those findings. The coordinators and judges would set up the stations ahead of time, organize the materials at each station in the same way, provide each team with the same directions, and inform the teams of how the event is to be scored. And, because it would be a timed event, you would inform students of the time allowed. As well, judges and students would need to know that, in scoring the activity, the identification of each of the powders would have some point value (perhaps 15 points per powder). Points would be subtracted for powders not identified, and points added for evidence presented in identifying the powders. For example, points could be distributed in this manner:

- identification of powders (15 points)
- powders missed (minus 2 points for each)
- evidence presented for identified powders (15 points)
- communication skills (5 points)

You might plan any number of events from other programs such as these.

- "Investigating Pendulums" from the Addison-Wesley Science Series.
- "Finding the Volume of the Sponge Without the Holes" from the Houghton Mifflin Science Program.
- "Rolling Cylinders" from Science: A Process Approach.
- "Identification of Environmental Factors" from the Science Curriculum Improvement Study.

One Olympic Challenge

Mass movement based on the SCIS program is perfect for fifth and sixth

Team	Trial 1 Goal: 23 cm	Trial 2 Goal: ___ cm	Trial 3 Goal: ___ cm	Total Team Score
School No. 1	Actual: 26.5 cm Score: 93	Actual: ___ cm Score: ___	Actual: ___ cm Score: ___	
School No. 2	Actual: ___ cm Score: ___	Actual: ___ cm Score: ___	Actual: ___ cm Score: ___	

Figure 1. **Score Sheet**

grade students. Participants (teams of two or three) take the prepared collection materials—spheres, a ramp, a metric tape, and a target mass. Their task is to move the target mass a given distance using the spheres and the ramp. After a 10- to 15-minute period, leaders tell the teams a specific distance that they must move their target mass. After a 2-minute preparation period (no practice runs), all teams release the spheres on command, and the distance is recorded by the judges. The procedure is repeated two more times, each time with a new distance. The winning team is the one with the least amount of error. Each team will need the following materials for this event:

- four spheres (one large metal, one small metal, one glass, and one wooden)
- a ramp with markings
- a target mass

You will also need

- 4–8 metric tapes (1 or 2 m long)
- a roll of masking tape (for starting lines)
- 5–10 pencils
- whistle
- 4 score sheets (See Figure 1.)
- clipboard

All participants must observe the following rules and procedure:

1. Participants may use only the materials provided.
2. Participants may gather and record data during the 10- to 15-minute investigation period. They may organize the data on paper any way they wish.
3. Once the investigation period is over, participants may not practice or manipulate the materials without instructions from the judges. A violation results in disqualification.
4. After the judges give the distance for moving the target mass, the participants may set up the ramp, select the sphere or spheres they plan to use, calculate which mark on the ramp should be the starting point for the spheres, and place the target mass on the starting line at the bottom of the ramp. (Participants may also shield their ramp from the direct view of other teams.)
5. Once the spheres are in place, the judges will give the signal to "release spheres." Participants will release the spheres and allow them to roll down, striking the target mass.
6. Participants must remain behind the starting line until the judges have recorded the data for ALL target masses.
7. Each team will have only one release per trial if the target mass or sphere(s)

does not function properly; the score for that trial will be zero.

Scoring for this event will be done as follows:

1. Measurements are made from the starting line to the back edge of the target mass using the metric tape. Measurements should be recorded to the nearest 0.5 cm.
2. Each measurement starts with 100 points, which would be given for a target mass that stops exactly at the distance given by the judges. For each 0.5 cm over or under the distance, 1 point is subtracted from the 100 points. For example, the distance given by the judges is 23 cm. The actual distance the target mass moved is 26.5 cm. The total distance over is 3.5 cm, equaling 7 penalty points, or a team score of 93 for the first trial. After the third trial, the scores for all three trials are totaled and winning positions are based on the highest total points for the event.

A Job Well Done

Since student recognition is an important objective of the elementary science challenge, you should present all participating students with certificates. As well, you might give ribbons in each category for first, second, and third places and announce each team's total score—thereby acknowledging each participating teacher, class, and school. Remind judges that student recognition is important in the challenge. In cases in which student results are very close, judges should reward each student.

In any case, the most rewarding thing for students will be the recognition of their efforts and the excitement that they have learned something new from the science challenge.

Donald E. Maxwell is assistant director of science, health, and outdoor education for Oakland Schools, Pontiac, Michigan. Glenn Berkheimer is a professor of science education at Michigan State University, East Lansing. Artwork by John Sinnett.

Appendix

Notes to parents, schedules for students, instructions to judges are the keystones science fair organizers rely upon. We've collected these forms for you to use as is, or to modify to meet your program's special needs. Most of these forms were originally produced by Ed Donovan of the School of Education, University of South Carolina, Spartansburg. We hope they will help you create the best science fair ever.

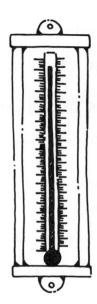

DAILY LOG

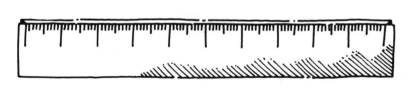

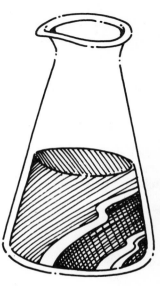

Science Fair Project Application

Name _____ Date _____

Teacher _____ Grade_____

Project Title _____

Project Description (be brief) _____

_____

_____

PROJECT AREA (circle one):

Biology   Chemistry   Physics   Mathematics   Behavioral   General Science

PROJECT TYPE (check one):

_____ *Experimental*—Forming a hypothesis (question) about something the student doesn't know the
answer to, doing an actual scientific experiment, making observations, collecting data, and reaching conclusions.

_____ *Demonstration*—Science in a show and tell format. The student knows what is going to happen when
he or she begins. Includes models, kits, collections, posters, etc.

_____ *Biological*—A project involving living things such as insects, birds, food, people, diseases, etc.

_____ *Physical*—A project involving things not living such as chemicals, stars, air pressure, weather, etc.

Will you require electricity? _____ YES   _____ NO

Your project should include the following items:

1. Exhibit that can stand by itself.
2. Research paper with bibliography.
3. Abstract (one page summary, with bibliography).
4. Materials necessary for the exhibit.
5. Oral presentation (3 to 5 minutes).
6. Logbook of daily work.

Return this completed form to your teacher by_____

Student signature_____

Parent's signature_____

Teacher's signature_____

Information for Students About Science Fair Projects

A Successful Science Project:

1. Represents your work—not that of an expert or your parents
2. Indicates an understanding of the science area chosen
3. Shows careful planning that would eliminate a "rush" project
4. Has a notebook showing a complete record of all your work
5. Has a simple, well-stated title and neat lettering
6. Includes photographs, charts, pictures, graphs, etc., that might be necessary to explain your work
7. Has accurate, valid, and correct observations
8. Tells a complete story—Problem and Solution
9. Is original in approach and presentation
10. Is self-explanatory
11. Is attractive and organized
12. Does not have to cost much money
13. Is best if it is an experiment, but it doesn't have to be
14. Is one that gives credit to those who gave help

A Science Fair Project is Not:

1. Only a report
2. Necessarily a new discovery or an original piece of research
3. Constructing a plastic model from a hobby kit
4. An enlarged model or drawing
5. A week-end chore
6. One, two, or even three posters
7. Something done by your parents or teacher

Steps in Making a Science Project:

1. Choose a topic and discuss it with your teacher. Ask your teacher for help and suggestions.
2. Once you have chosen your topic problem, find out as much about the topic a possible.
3. Keep a project notebook and record all of your thought, preparations, and ideas. Keep a record of your readings.
4. Set up a work area somewhere around your house where you can work on your project. Make sure the area is off limits to your pets or younger brothers and sisters.
5. Work on your project a little each day, don't wait until the last minute.
6. Collect the materials needed for the project.
7. Check with your teacher for suggestions and materials, he or she can save you time, excess, work, and money.
8. Construct your exhibit and make letters for your signs.
9. Mount your pictures, graphs, charts, etc.
10. Present your science project at the fair.

Created by Becky Brown, Chapman Elementary School, Spartanburg School District #7, Spartanburg, South Carolina
Modified by Ed Donovan, Science Education Center, School of Education, University of South Carolina, Spartanburg

Schedule for the Student's Science Fair Project

Week	What You Should Be Working On	Due Date	Check ✓
1	* Make sure you understand what you need to do for the science fair project. Ask questions if you're not certain about any aspect of the assignment. * Find time to use books, encyclopedias, and magazines at the library. Look for a topic that is interesting to you. Keep bibliographic notes on the books and magazine articles where you get your ideas. * You may want to visit museums, hospitals, universities, zoos, and science centers to get ideas.		
2	* With your project idea firmly in mind, write the purpose, question, hypothesis, materials needed, and procedures. * Show your written material to the teacher and discuss your project for approval.		
3	* After the science project has been approved by the science teacher, begin to gather your necessary equipment and begin your project.		
4	* Seek advice and help from professionals to refine your project: doctors, nurses, researchers, teachers, librarians, veterinarians.		
5	* Conduct your experiment and collect data. * Keep careful, written records of results in a notebook. Record the day and time you make observations. Be as specific as you can about the amount, size, and type of materials, plants, or animals you use.		
6	* Draw conclusion and organize the results of your experiments in chart or graph form.		
7	* Write your research paper. Include a table of contents, abstract, summary sheet, purpose or hypothesis, step-by-step explanation of your experiment, results, conclusion, and bibliography.		
8	* Construct your exhibit. Build a back-drop to mount graphs, charts, illustrations, photographs, signs, and summary sheets.		
9	* Prepare an oral presentation.		
10	* Add finishing touches to your project. * Come to the science fair and present your project.		

The Scientific Method

A student record sheet for an experiment or science project

1. What do you want to find out?
   (PURPOSE)

2. What do you think will happen?
   (HYPOTHESIS)

3. What do you need to use?
   (MATERIALS)

4. What will you do to find out?
   (PROCEDURES)

5. What happened?
   (RESULTS)

6. What did you learn?
   (CONCLUSIONS)

Note to Parents

We hope the following suggestions will be helpful as your child develops this year's science project:

1. Please remember that the most important ingredient in any project is the amount of work the student accomplishes, how much knowledge he or she acquires, and how much initiative is displayed. Many abilities are developed researching, organizing, outlining, measuring, calculating, reporting, and presenting. These involve the reading, writing, arithmetic, and social skills so much a part of successful daily living.

2. Although it is to be the student's effort, there is no substitute for a parent's support.

3. Do not worry about the project's performance at a science fair. If strengthened thinking skills and increased knowledge have occurred, then a prize has truly been won.

4. Areas in which a parent's assistance will be necessary include:
   a. *Safety*. Be sure that poisons, dangerous chemicals, and open fires are avoided. Learn and practice electrical safety if electricity is used in the project. If any aspect of the project appears to be dangerous, it is not to be included.
   b. *Transportation*. Help will be needed for the transportation of materials to the science fair, although it is better if the student can set up and take down the exhibit with a minimum of assistance.

5. Areas in which a parent's assistance may be welcome include:
   a. Suggesting project ideas (these may be connected with your work).
   b. Transportation to libraries, businesses, museums, nature centers, universities, or any source of project information.
   c. Technical work such as construction and photography.
   d. Being an interested listener.

Reprinted with permission from Public Service Company of New Mexico, Educational Programs, Alvarado Square, Albuquerque, New Mexico 87158. © PNM 1982

- -

Science Fair Parent Volunteer Form

I would like to volunteer for the following jobs at the science fair:
(Check where you can help.)

_____ Science Fair Committee   _____ Supervise students setting up

_____ Help set up the gym   _____ Supervise students during judging

_____ Help supply refreshments   _____ Help clean up the gym

Name_____ Addresss_____

Telephone #_____ **PLEASE RETURN BY**_____

Helping Your Children with <u>Their</u> Science Fair Projects

Things a parent may do:

1. Give encouragement, support, and guidance. (Be positive!)
2. Make sure your child feels it is his or her project. Make sure the project is primarily the work of the child.
3. Realize that the main purpose of a science fair project is to help your child use and strengthen the basic skills he or she has learned and to develop higher level skills.
4. Realize your child will need help in understanding, acquiring, and using the major science process skills (researching, organizing, measuring, calculating, reporting, demonstrating, experimenting, collecting, constructing, presenting). Your child may not have been taught these skills. Therefore, it may not be fair to expect him or her to know how to do them.
5. Realize that your child may be using reading, writing, arithmetic, and social skills for the first time in a creative way to solve a problem.
6. Realize that the teacher works with 20-30 students and this may make it difficult to give a large amount of individual attention to your child.
7. Understand that the teacher may need your help. If you have the interest and the time, you might contact the teacher and volunteer to help or judge at the school's science fair.
8. Help your child plan a mutually agreed upon schedule, to prevent a last minute project and a disrupted household. A 4 to 8 week plan that uses a check-off sheet is best. The following steps (you may want to add more) should be on your schedule.
   a. find a topic.
   b. narrow down the topic to a specific scientific problem that is appropriate to the child's ability level.
   c. research what is already known about the problem.
   d. develop a hypothesis. (What outcome do you expect?)
   e. develop a procedure/investigation to test the hypothesis (if experimental).
   f. make observations and collecting appropriate data.
   g. interpret the data and other observations.
   h. state and display the results.
   i. draw appropriate conclusions.
   j. create the exhibit.
   k. write the research paper and the abstract.
   l. present the project.
9. Help your child design a safe project that is not hazardous in any way.
10. Provide transportation to such places as libraries, nature centers, universities, etc. that can help the child find project information.

11. Help your child write letters to people who can provide help on the science project and be sure the letters are mailed.

12. Help the child develop the necessary technical skills and/or help the child do the technical work such as building the exhibit and doing the photography.

13. Help your child understand that science is not a subject but a "way of looking at the world around us."

14. Be sure that the child states in the paper and/or exhibit the help he or she has received from you or others. This will help judges to make a fairer evaluation of the project.

15. Look over the project to check for good grammar, neatness, spelling, and accuracy. Make suggestions on how it can be corrected .

16. Buy or help find the necessary materials to complete the project.

17. Realize that a good project doesn't have to cost a lot of money. Many times a simple project that is well displayed and explained is the best.

18. Help the child understand that a weekend chore, or one or two posters, is not a project.

19. Help the child to keep a record (log book) of all he or she does and a list of references used.

20. Find an area in the house where the child can work on the project and not have to worry about pets or brothers and sisters.

21. Explain to the child that he or she should consult with you or the teacher when problems arise. Set aside time for help sessions. Make them short and constructive. Be an interested and enthusiastic listener.

22. Have your child present his or her science project to you before he or she takes it to school.

23. Help transport child and the science fair project to and from the school/district/regional science fairs.

24. Do not worry or get upset if your child doesn't win a prize at the science fair. The skills the child has gained are worth all of the effort. Help your child to begin to plan for next year.

25. Feel a sense of pride and satisfaction when the project and the science fair are finished. Share this with your child, you have both earned it.

Science Fair Project Judging Criteria

Scientific Thought (30 points)

Does the project follow the scientific method? (hypothesis, method, data, conclusion)
Is the problem clearly and concisely stated?
Are the procedures appropriate, organized, and thorough?
Is the information collected accurate and complete?
Does the study illustrate a controlled experiment that makes appropriate comparisons?
Are the variables clearly defined?
Are the conclusions accurate and based upon the results?
Does the project show the child is familiar with the topic?
Does the project represent real study and effort?

Creative Ability (30 points)

How unique is the project?
Does the exhibit show original thinking or a unique method or approach?
Is it significant and unusual for the age of the student?
Does the project demonstrate ideas arrived by the child?

Understanding (10 points)

Does it explain what the student learned about the topic?
Did the student use appropriate literature for research?
Is a list of references or bibliography available?
In the exhibit, did the student tell a complete and concise story, and answer
 some questions about the topic?

Clarity (10 points)

Did the student clearly communicate the nature of the problem, how the problem
 was solved, and the conclusions?
Are the problems, procedures, data, and conclusions presented clearly, and in
 a logical order?
Did the student clearly and accurately articulate in writing what was accomplished?
Is the objective of the project likely to be understood by one not trained in the subject area?

Dramatic Value (10 points)

How well did the student design and construct the exhibit?
Are all of the components of the project done well? (exhibit, paper, abstract, log of work)
Is the proper emphasis given to important ideas?
Is the display visually appealing?
Is attention sustained by the project and focused on the objective?

Technical Skill (10 points)

Was the majority of the work done by the student, and was it done at home or in school?
Does the project show effort and good craftsmanship by the student?
Has the student acknowledged help received from others?
Does the written material show attention to grammar and to spelling?
Is the project physically sound and durably constructed? Will it stand normal wear and tear?
Does the project stand by itself?

Science Fair Project Judging Form

Project Title _____   Project Number _____

Project Category _____   Judge Number _____

CRITERIA: POINTS

Scientific Thought (30 Points)   _____
    Is the problem concisely stated?
    Are the procedures appropriate and thorough?
    Is the information collected complete?
    Are the conclusions reached accurate?
    Comments:

Creativity (30 points)   _____
    How unique is the project?
    Is it significant and unusual for the age of the student?
    Does the project show ideas arrived by the student?
    Comments:

Understanding (10 points)   _____
    What did the student learn about the project?
    Did the student use appropriate literature for research?
    Can the student answer questions about the topic?
    Comments:

Clarity (10 points)   _____
    Are the problems, procedures, data, and conclusions presented logically?
    Can the _objective_ be understood by non-scientists?
    Is the written material clear and articulate?
    Comments:

Dramatic Value (10 points)   _____
    How well did the student present the project?
    Is the display visually appealing?
    Is the proper emphasis given to important ideas?
    Comments:

Technical Skill (10 points)   _____
    Was the majority of the work done by the student?
    Does the written material show attention to grammar and spelling?
    Is the project well-constructed?
    Comments:

TOTAL POINTS
(based upon 100)   _____

Notes

Notes

Notes

Notes

Notes

This volume has been produced by
  NSTA Special Publications
  Phyllis Marcuccio, Director of Publications
  Shirley Watt, Managing Editor
  Crystal Hamann, Assistant Editor
  Diana Holmes, Editorial Assistant
  Peter Andersen, Editorial Assistant